Current
CONTROVERSIES

Enhanced Interrogation and Torture

Other Books in the Current Controversies Series

Enhanced Interrogation and Torture

Gary Wiener, Book Editor

GREENHAVEN
PUBLISHING

Published in 2018 by Greenhaven Publishing, LLC
353 3rd Avenue, Suite 255, New York, NY 10010

Articles in Greenhaven Publishing anthologies are often edited for length to meet page
requirements. In addition, original titles of these works are changed to clearly present
the main thesis and to explicitly indicate the author's opinion. Every effort is made to
ensure that Greenhaven Publishing accurately reflects the original intent of the authors.
Every effort has been made to trace the owners of the copyrighted material.

Cover image: palidachan/Shutterstock.com

Library of Congress Cataloging-in-Publication Data

Names: Wiener, Gary, editor.
Title: Enhanced interrogation and torture / Gary Wiener, book editor.
Description: New York : Greenhaven Publishing, LLC, [2018] | Series: Current
   controversies | Includes bibliographical references and index. | Audience: Grades 9–12.
Identifiers: LCCN 2017041742| ISBN 9781534502352 (library bound) | ISBN
   9781534502413 (pbk.)
Subjects: LCSH: United States. Central Intelligence Agency. | Intelligence
   service—Methodology. | Military interrogation—United States. |
   Terrorism—United States—Prevention.
Classification: LCC JK468.I6 .E65 2018 | DDC 327.1273--dc23
LC record available at https://lccn.loc.gov/2017041742

Manufactured in the United States of America

Website: http://greenhavenpublishing.com

Contents

Human Rights First

After 9/11, the CIA was authorized to use a variety of "enhanced interrogation" techniques to glean information from adversaries of the United States. These techniques included waterboarding, sleep deprivation, solitary confinement, stress positions, and much more.

Justin Scuiletti

A US Senate report claimed that the CIA Enhanced Interrogation Program was brutal and ineffective, but the CIA director argued that the program aided the capture of al-Qaeda operatives, foiled some terrorist plots, and increased US knowledge of al-Qaeda operations.

Robert Siegel and Peter Hoekstra

A former chairman of the Senate Intelligence Committee defends the enhanced interrogation program, claiming that it helped the United States more effectively combat the threat of radical jihadism.

ThinkProgress

In this group of observations collected by the organization ThinkProgress, a wide range of experts, from American general David Petraeus to army intelligence officers and FBI special agents, all claim that enhanced interrogation does not yield valuable results.

Chapter 2: Is Enhanced Interrogation Morally Defensible?

Yes: Sometimes the Ends Justify the Means

Chapter 3: Is Enhanced Interrogation Just Another Name for Torture?

that enhanced interrogation is wrong and may encourage other nations to act outside of the law.

Yes: Enhanced Interrogation, Unlike Torture, Is Not Illegal

Ted Lapkin

Terrorists are illegal combatants whose actions do not conform to the rule of law. Therefore, the Geneva Conventions do not apply to them, and to give them such protections as afforded by international law would be both a legal and moral mistake.

John A. Rizzo

The chief legal officer for the CIA defends his decision to legally authorize enhanced interrogation techniques and asserts that the CIA did not decide to use enhanced interrogation techniques rashly or even enthusiastically.

No: Enhanced Interrogation Is a Violation of International Law

William Taft IV

Regulations on torture have already been resolved under the Geneva Conventions and under the United States Army Field Manual guidelines. The US should leave things where they are and not look to new methods.

Rebecca Gordon

During the 2016 Republican debates, candidates presented their opinions about how tough they would be on terrorism. Many of their suggestions crossed the boundary into the realm of war crimes.

Foreword

"Controversy" is a word that has an undeniably unpleasant connotation. It carries a definite negative charge. Controversy can spoil family gatherings, spread a chill around classroom and campus discussion, inflame public discourse, open raw civic wounds, and lead to the ouster of public officials. We often feel that controversy is almost akin to bad manners, a rude and shocking eruption of that which must not be spoken or thought of in polite, tightly guarded society. To avoid controversy, to quell controversy, is often seen as a public good, a victory for etiquette, perhaps even a moral or ethical imperative.

Yet the studious, deliberate avoidance of controversy is also a whitewashing, a denial, a death threat to democracy. It is a false sterilizing and sanitizing and superficial ordering of the messy, ragged, chaotic, at times ugly processes by which a healthy democracy identifies and confronts challenges, engages in passionate debate about appropriate approaches and solutions, and arrives at something like a consensus and a broadly accepted and supported way forward. Controversy is the megaphone, the speaker's corner, the public square through which the citizenry finds and uses its voice. Controversy is the lifeblood of our democracy and absolutely essential to the vibrant health of our society.

Our present age is certainly no stranger to controversy. We are consumed by fierce debates about technology, privacy, political correctness, poverty, violence, crime and policing, guns, immigration, civil and human rights, terrorism, militarism, environmental protection, and gender and racial equality. Loudly competing voices are raised every day, shouting opposing opinions, putting forth competing agendas, and summoning starkly different visions of a utopian or dystopian future. Often these voices attempt to shout the others down; there is precious little listening and considering among the cacophonous din. Yet listening and considering, too, are essential to the health of a democracy. If controversy is democracy's lusty lifeblood, respectful listening and careful thought are its higher faculties, its brain, its conscience.

Current Controversies does not shy away from or attempt to hush the loudly competing voices. It seeks to provide readers with as wide and representative as possible a range of articulate voices on any given controversy of the day, separates each one out to allow it to be heard clearly and fairly, and encourages careful listening to each of these well-crafted, thoughtfully expressed opinions, supplied by some of today's leading academics, thinkers, analysts, politicians, policy makers, economists, activists, change agents, and advocates. Only after listening to a wide range of opinions on an issue, evaluating the strengths and weaknesses of each argument, assessing how well the facts and available evidence mesh with the stated opinions and conclusions, and thoughtfully and critically examining one's own beliefs and conscience can the reader begin to arrive at his or her own conclusions and articulate his or her own stance on the spotlighted controversy.

This process is facilitated and supported in each Current Controversies volume by an introduction and chapter overviews that provide readers with the essential context they need to begin engaging with the spotlighted controversies, with the debates surrounding them, and with their own perhaps shifting or nascent opinions on them. Chapters are organized around several key questions that are answered with diverse opinions representing all points on the political spectrum. In its content, organization, and methodology, readers are encouraged to determine the authors' point of view and purpose, interrogate and analyze the various arguments and their rhetoric and structure, evaluate the arguments' strengths and weaknesses, test their claims against available facts and evidence, judge the validity of the reasoning, and bring into clearer, sharper focus the reader's own beliefs and conclusions and how they may differ from or align with those in the collection or those of classmates.

Research has shown that reading comprehension skills improve dramatically when students are provided with compelling, intriguing, and relevant "discussable" texts. The subject matter of these collections could not be more compelling, intriguing, or urgently relevant to today's students and the world they are poised to inherit. The anthologized articles also provide the basis for stimulating, lively, and passionate classroom debates. Students who are compelled to anticipate objections to their own argument and identify the flaws in those of an opponent read more carefully, think more critically, and steep themselves in relevant context, facts, and information more thoroughly. In short, using discussable text of the kind provided by every single volume in the Current Controversies series encourages close reading, facilitates reading comprehension, fosters research, strengthens critical thinking, and greatly enlivens and energizes classroom discussion and participation. The entire learning process is deepened, extended, and strengthened.

If we are to foster a knowledgeable, responsible, active, and engaged citizenry, we must provide readers with the intellectual, interpretive, and critical-thinking tools and experience necessary to make sense of the world around them and the all-important debates and arguments that inform it. We must encourage them not to run away from or attempt to quell controversy but to embrace it in a responsible, conscientious, and thoughtful way, to sharpen and strengthen their own informed opinions by listening to and critically analyzing those of others. This series encourages respectful engagement with and analysis of current controversies and competing opinions and fosters a resulting increase in the strength and rigor of one's own opinions and stances. As such, it helps readers assume their rightful place in the public square and provides them with the skills necessary to uphold their awesome responsibility—guaranteeing the continued and future health of a vital, vibrant, and free democracy.

Introduction

Among the dubious techniques the United States has used to fight the "war on terror," including drone attacks and assassination, none has been more controversial than enhanced interrogation. In the aftermath of al-Qaeda's 9/11 attacks on the United States, then-president George W. Bush authorized the use of such interrogation techniques in an attempt to gain intelligence about future terrorist strikes. These techniques have included waterboarding, subjection to extreme temperatures, stress positions (putting the body in uncomfortable positions for long periods of time), confinement to small boxes, and more. Such forms of abuse are uncomfortable for the average American to consider, and so the Bush administration invented a euphemism, a nicer way of talking about what is, to many, nothing less than torture. That euphemism is "enhanced interrogation."

While enhanced interrogation has been a topic of controversy in the twenty-first century, the concept did not originate with the war on terror. In a 2014 report on enhanced interrogation, the Senate Intelligence Committee found that US intelligence had a history of using coercive intelligence. In 1963, a manual referred to as KUBARK detailed numerous extreme interrogation techniques that were used on information-rich subjects such as Soviet double agents and Latin American dissidents.

But such methods have come under fire even from members of the intelligence community. Upon investigating the use of forced standing and sensory deprivation on a Soviet KGB officer, CIA officer John Limond Hart remarked that such tactics were "an abomination, and I am happy to say that it is...not typical of what my colleagues and I did in the agency during the time I was connected to it."[1] Nevertheless, it is now known that some of the same intelligence officers who adopted harsh interrogation techniques in Latin America in the 1980s "were key players" in setting up the enhanced interrogation of the 2000s.[2] Some of these techniques were apparently learned from the practices of North Vietnamese Communist interrogators who used them to extract information for propaganda purposes from American prisoners during the Vietnam War.

The United States has often justified enhanced interrogation as a means of fighting fire with fire. The often heinous and barbaric practices of groups such as al-Qaeda and ISIS warrant, to some in US intelligence, the use of equally harsh measures. Others in the CIA have balked at taking such liberties with international law, which forbids the use of torture. They worry about the United States giving up the moral high ground that many in the country hold dear.

In particular, photos from the Abu Ghraib prison showing US Army soldiers abusing Iraqi prisoners shocked Americans when they were released in April 2004 and made many in the United States question whether the US really was the "good guy" in the Middle East. When CIA members were questioned as to whether they used similar techniques their response was that the army, not the intelligence community, had committed these atrocities. But this response was an evasion. US intelligence had and would continue to use enhanced interrogation against Middle Eastern prisoners.

Central to the enhanced interrogation debate is the idea of whether or not it is really torture, which would constitute a violation of international law. Liberals usually insist that it is and conservatives that it is not. But Republican senator John McCain, who was himself subjected to torture in Vietnam, has repeatedly argued against enhanced interrogation, and fellow Republican Ron Paul agreed: "Waterboarding is torture," he said.[3] On the other hand, in November of 2016, Republican senator Tom Cotton told CNN's Wolf Blitzer that waterboarding was not torture and that then president-elect Donald Trump was prepared to reverse Obama-era policy and use waterboarding and "much worse" to extract information from terrorists: "We have to play the game the way they're playing the game. You're not going to win if we're soft and they're, they have no rules," Trump told CBS's *Face The Nation*.[4]

One's opinion on the subject varies according to one's experiences. Northwestern University professor Loren Nordgren has found that "Psychologists have discovered that people who aren't enduring a painful experience have a hard time estimating just how painful it is. This finding is known as an empathy gap."[5] This may account for why McCain considers enhanced interrogation tactics to be torture and why Cotton does not.

Still another controversy is whether enhanced interrogation actually works. Here, too, opinion is divided. President Trump has explicitly stated that torture "absolutely works."[6] On the other hand, the FBI director he fired in the spring of 2017, James Comey, stated in testimony before the US Senate that torture is "also ineffective, frankly, but that's a whole other deal."[7] The Senate's 2014 report on enhanced interrogation concluded "use of the CIA's enhanced interrogation techniques was not an effective means of obtaining accurate information or gaining detainee cooperation." In fact, the report stated, subjects of enhanced interrogation often provided "fabricated information."[8] Trump, on the other hand, in a campaign stump speech before the presidential election of 2016, insisted that he had spoken to experts on the subject and that "only a stupid person would say that it [enhanced interrogation] doesn't work."[9] Trinity College (Dublin) Professor Shane O'Mara, author of the book *Why Torture Doesn't Work: The Neuroscience of Interrogation*, was puzzled by Trump's remarks. He wondered about Trump's source of information on the subject. "With Trump it's very difficult to know who he has been talking to," O'Mara told CNN.[10] And while Trump has gone after groups such as ISIS somewhat more aggressively than his predecessor, Obama, no news of the actual use of enhanced interrogation techniques had leaked out early in his presidency.

Regardless, enhanced interrogation techniques will continue to be a hotly debated subject among politicians, intelligence operatives, military personnel, and the public. In *Current Controversies:*

Enhanced Interrogation and Torture, various experts debate the pros and cons of extreme interrogation techniques, providing a wide range of opinions that are sure to enlighten the reader about this complex and thorny issue.

Notes

1. Jeff Stein, "CIA 'Torture' Practices Started Long Before 9/11 Attacks." *Newsweek.*

2. Loren Nordgren, "Waterboarding Isn't Torture? Try It." CNN. November 16, 2011. http://www.cnn.com/2011/11/16/opinion/nordgren-waterboarding/index.html

3. Ibid.

4. Christina Manduley, "Senator Tom Cotton: Waterboarding Isn't Torture." CNN. November 9, 2016. http://www.cnn.com/2016/11/09/politics/tom-cotton-waterboarding-torture/

5. Nordgren, "Waterboarding isn't torture? Try It." CNN.

6. James Masters, Donald Trump says torture "absolutely works"—but does it?" CNN. January 26, 2017. http://www.cnn.com/2017/01/26/politics/donald-trump-torture-waterboarding/index.html

7. Washington Post Staff, "Read the Full Testimony of FBI Director James Comey in Which He Discusses Clinton Email Investigation." *Washington Post.* May 3, 2017. https://www.washingtonpost.com/news/post-politics/wp/2017/05/03/read-the-full-testimony-of-fbi-director-james-comey-in-which-he-discusses-clinton-email-investigation/?utm_term=.173b0df1a808

8. Masters, Donald Trump Says Torture "Absolutely Works"—but Does It?" CNN.

9. Ibid.

10. Ibid.

CHAPTER 1

Is Enhanced Interrogation of Enemies Justified?

Overview: An Introduction to Enhanced Interrogation

Human Rights First

Human Rights First is an independent advocacy and action organization that works around the world to harness American influence in an effort to secure core freedoms. It presses the US government and private companies to respect human rights and the rule of law.

The CIA's Detention and Interrogation Program allowed the use of so-called "enhanced interrogation techniques" on detainees captured after 9/11. It was conducted between 2002 and 2009, with the authorization of officials in the Bush Administration's White House and the Department of Justice. During that time, 119 detainees were held in CIA custody, and at least 39 were subjected to these techniques. These techniques constitute torture,[1] or cruel, inhuman or degrading treatment—both illegal under U.S. and international law. Several detainees were waterboarded, and the CIA often used combinations of tactics such as sleep deprivation of detainees kept in stress positions, or sensory deprivation of detainees who were shackled and in solitary confinement. This document explains what the so-called "enhanced interrogation" and related interrogation techniques are, and the physical and psychological effects of their use.

- Sleep deprivation. The detainees were kept awake by being shackled, forced to stand, or kept in stress positions in an attempt to destroy their capacity for psychological resistance. This was routinely combined with nudity and/or round-the-clock interrogation. Although not overtly violent, extended periods of sleep deprivation can have painful and damaging

"'Enhanced Interrogation' Explained," Human Rights First, February 10, 2016. Reprinted by permission.

mental and physical effects. After being forced to stand for 54 hours, Abu Ja'far al-Iraqi required blood thinners to treat the swelling in his legs. Following 56 hours without sleep, Arsala Khan suffered from violent hallucinations of dogs mauling and killing his family.

- Standing on broken feet. As an extreme form of sleep deprivation, two detainees, Abu Hazim and Abd al-Karim, were forced to stand for hours with broken feet. Despite recommendations that he avoid weight bearing for three months, Abu Hazim underwent 52 hours of standing sleep deprivation on his broken foot, barely a month after his diagnosis. While injured, these detainees were also subjected to walling.
- Solitary confinement. Detainees were regularly confined with no opportunity for social interaction. This was often combined with nudity, sensory deprivation, total darkness or constant light, and shackling. Abu Zubaydah was isolated naked in a cell with bright lights and white noise or loud music playing. At one point, he was kept for 47 days in total isolation. The dangers of solitary confinement were recognized by the United States Supreme Court as early as 1890 in In re Medley, where the Court described prisoners becoming violently insane, committing suicide, and the partial loss of their mental activity.[2]
- Stress positions. These positions are designed to cause pain and discomfort for extended periods of time, and were often used in combination with sleep deprivation. Detainees were shackled with their arms over their heads, forced to stay standing, or were placed in cramped confinement, such as coffin-sized boxes. Abd al-Rahim al-Nashiri was subjected to improvised stress positions that not only caused cuts and bruises but led to the intervention of a medical officer who was concerned al-Nashiri's shoulders would be dislocated. Abu Zubaydah was confined to a coffin-shaped box for a total of over 11 days.

- Rectal feeding and rectal exams. Rectal feeding was used for prisoners who refused food and entails the insertion of a tube containing pureed food into the detainee's anal passage. This was used for behavior control, without medical necessity, despite risks of damage to the colon and rectum, or of food rotting inside the digestive tract. One detainee, Mustafa Ahmed al-Hawsawi, suffered a rectal prolapse likely caused by overly-harsh rectal exams.
- Nudity. This form of sexual humiliation relies on cultural and religious taboos, and required detainees to be fully or partially naked during interrogations or when shackled. Nudity was also regularly combined with cold temperatures and cold showers. One detainee, Gul Rahman, died of suspected hypothermia following 48 hours of sleep deprivation, half-naked, in an extremely cold room.
- Threats. Detainees were threatened with further physical torture as well as violence, death or sexual abuse against their family. One CIA officer operated a cordless drill near Abd al-Rahim al-Nashiri's body while he was blindfolded. KSM was threatened with the death of his children and the abuse of his mother. Several instances of mock executions were also reported. Such threats have been shown to induce extreme fear and loss of control, recurring nightmares, and intrusive memories, which are strongly associated with PTSD and major depression.

References

1. 18 U.S. Code § 2340(1). The United States defines torture as "an act committed by a person acting under the color of law specifically intended to inflict severe physical or mental pain or suffering (other than pain or suffering incidental to lawful sanctions) upon another person within his custody or physical control." The severity of harm caused by an interrogation technique is key in determining whether it constitutes torture.

2. In re Medley, 134 U.S. 160 (1890).

Despite a Senate Report to the Contrary, Enhanced Interrogation Works

Justin Scuiletti

Justin Scuiletti is the digital video producer for PBS NewsHour, *for which he also writes stories.*

The Central Intelligence Agency's use of "enhanced interrogation techniques" was "not an effective means of acquiring intelligence or gaining cooperation from detainees," a Senate report claims.

The report on the CIA's use of interrogation, released by the Senate Intelligence Committee Tuesday, went into detail about several of the methods used.

Ten interrogation techniques were verbally approved by Attorney General John Ashcroft on July 24, 2002: "the attention grasp, walling, the facial hold, the facial slap (insult slap), cramped confinement, wall standing, stress positions, sleep deprivation, use of diapers, and use of insects" with the verbal approval of waterboarding given two days later. The report even describes other, unconventional methods of interrogations, such as the holding of an "intellectually challenged" man who was taped crying to be used as leverage to "get a family member to provide information."

The report described many of the interrogations that used these techniques as "brutal" and said there was no evidence of the agency first attempting alternative, "non-threatening" approaches before resorting to them:

> Beginning with the CIA's first detainee, Abu Zubaydah, and continuing with numerous others, the CIA applied its enhanced interrogation techniques with significant repetition for days

"Report: CIA's Enhanced Interrogation Techniques 'Brutal' and 'Ineffective,'" by Justin Scuiletti, NewsHour Productions LLC, December 9, 2014. Reprinted by permission © 2014 News Hour Productions LLC..

or weeks at a time. Interrogation techniques such as slaps and "wallings" (slamming detainees against a wall) were used in combination, frequently concurrent with sleep deprivation and nudity. Records do not support CIA representations that the CIA initially used an "an open, non- threatening approach," or that interrogations began with the "least coercive technique possible" and escalated to more coercive techniques only as necessary. (Senate Select Committee on Intelligence Report Executive Summary — Page 3)

The use of sleep deprivation was described to involve the forcing of detainees to remain awake for upwards of 180 hours, all while standing or in stressful positions; sometimes shackled. At least five detainees were said to have experienced "disturbing hallucinations," such as in the case of Arsala Khan in 2003, detailed on page 109 of the report. Khan, after 56 hours of standing sleep deprivation, could barely enunciate and was "visibly shaken by his hallucinations depicting dogs mauling and killing his sons and family."

Waterboarding, the effect of which is described as inducing the sensation of drowning, was noted to have resulted instead in a "series of near drownings" when used on Abu Zubaydah and Khalid Sheikh Mohammed, referred to here as "KSM":

According to CIA records, Abu Zubaydah's waterboarding sessions "resulted in immediate fluid intake and involuntary leg, chest and arm spasms" and "hysterical pleas." A medical officer who oversaw the interrogation of KSM stated that the waterboard technique had evolved beyond the "sensation of drowning" to what he described as a "series of near drownings." Physical reactions to waterboarding did not necessarily end when the application of water was discontinued, as both Abu Zubaydah and KSM vomited after being subjected to the waterboard. Further, as previously described, during at least one waterboard session, Abu Zubaydah "became completely unresponsive, with bubbles rising through his open, full mouth." (page 423)

The report also called into question the agency's collection of "unique" information from detainees using these interrogation methods. The CIA, the report also alleges, purposely omitted the amount of relevant information gained from other methods outside those interrogations, giving the "false impression the CIA was acquiring unique information from the use of the techniques."

An example given, purportedly drawing from CIA records, says that seven of 39 detainees that were known to have been subjected to the enhanced interrogation techniques from the agency but "produced no intelligence while in CIA custody." The report stated that several detainees "provided significant accurate intelligence prior to, or without having been subjected to these techniques."

For examples, the report returns to the cases of Zubaydah and KSM. For Zubaydah, information allegedly gained from the enhanced techniques, including the identification of KSM as the mastermind of the Sept. 11, 2001 attacks, are instead attributed by the report to interrogations conducted before the use of the enhanced interrogation:

> According to CIA records, Abu Zubaydah provided information on "al-Qa'ida activities, plans, capabilities, and relationships," in addition to information on "its leadership structure, including personalities, decision-making processes, training, and tactics." This type of information was provided by Abu Zubaydah prior to, during, and after the use of the CIA's enhanced interrogation techniques. At no point during or after the use of the CIA's enhanced interrogation techniques did Abu Zubaydah provide information on al-Qa'ida cells in the United States or operational plans for terrorist attacks against the United States. Further, a quantitative review of Abu Zubaydah's intelligence reporting indicates that more intelligence reports were disseminated from Abu Zubaydah's first two months of interrogation, before the use of the CIA's enhanced interrogation techniques and when FBI special agents were directly participating, than were derived during the next two-month phase of interrogations, which included the non-stop use of the CIA's enhanced interrogation techniques 24 hours a day for 17 days. (page 208)

The report draws from an April 12, 2007, CIA testimony by Michael Hayden—then-director of the CIA—to point out supposed inaccuracies in CIA claims of enhanced interrogation effectiveness by comparing statements from Hayden to CIA interrogation records. Where Hayden stated that waterboarding was successful in retrieving information from Khalid Sheikh Mohammed, records state that CIA personnel even believed that the use of waterboarding on KSM was "ineffective" claiming that one of his interrogators suggested that non-confrontational approaches had been much more successful.

> CIA personnel—including members of KSM's interrogation team —believed that the waterboard interrogation technique was ineffective on KSM. The on-site medical officer told the inspector general that, after three or four days, it became apparent that the waterboard was ineffective, and that KSM "hated it but knew he could manage." KSM interrogator [redacted] told the inspector general that KSM had "beat the system," and assessed two months after the discontinuation of the waterboard that KSM responded to "creature comforts and sense of importance" and not to "confrontational" approaches. (page 313)

In addition to the supposed ineffectiveness of waterboarding on Khalid Sheikh Mohammed, the report also alleges that KSM gave inaccurate statements to interrogators because of the enhanced interrogation:

> The CIA repeatedly represented that KSM had "recanted little of the information" he had provided, and that KSM's information was "generally accurate" and "consistent." This assertion is not supported by CIA records. Throughout the period during which KSM was subjected to the CIA's enhanced interrogation techniques, KSM provided inaccurate information, much of which he would later acknowledge was fabricated and recant. (page 213)

Accuracy was also called into question concerning the interrogations of Ramzi bin al-Shibh, an associate of Khalid Sheikh Mohammed:

Much of [bin al-Shibh's] statements on the 11 September attacks have been speculative, and many of the details could be found in media accounts of the attacks that appeared before he was detained. In the few instances where his reporting was unique and plausible, we cannot verify or refute the information... he has been sketchy on some aspects of the 9/11 plot, perhaps in order to downplay his role in the plot. His information on individuals is non specific; he has given us nothing on the Saudi hijackers or others who played a role... The overall quality of his reporting has steadily declined since 2003. (page 80)

Several have disputed the Senate Intelligence Committee's claims that the techniques were ineffective. In a statement released Tuesday, CIA Director John Brennan said that, though the CIA found some common ground with the report's findings, the agency did not agree on several points. "Our review indicates that interrogations of detainees on whom EITs were used did produce intelligence that helped thwart attack plans, capture terrorists, and save lives," the statement said. "The intelligence gained from the program was critical to our understanding of al Qaida and continues to inform our counterterrorism efforts to this day."

Former CIA directors George Tenet, Porter Goss and Michael Hayden and former CIA Deputy Directors John McLaughlin, Albert Calland and Stephen Kappes—writing in The Wall Street Journal—said that the program led to the capture of senior al Qaida operatives, disrupted several terrorist plots and added to the overall knowledge of how al Qaida operates.

The article claims that without the use of the enhanced interrogation techniques on Abu Zubaydah and Ramzi bin al-Shibh, Khalid Sheikh Mohammed would never have been captured. Without using the interrogation program on KSM, they also claim, further al Qaida associates would not have been apprehended:

A powerful example of the interrogation program's importance is the information obtained from Abu Zubaydah, a senior al Qaeda operative, and from Khalid Sheikh Muhammed, known as KSM, the 9/11 mastermind. We are convinced that both would not have talked absent the interrogation program.

Information provided by Zubaydah through the interrogation program led to the capture in 2002 of KSM associate and post-9/11 plotter Ramzi Bin al-Shibh. Information from both Zubaydah and al-Shibh led us to KSM. KSM then led us to Riduan Isamuddin, aka Hambali, East Asia's chief al Qaeda ally and the perpetrator of the 2002 Bali bombing in Indonesia—in which more than 200 people perished.

The removal of these senior al Qaeda operatives saved thousands of lives because it ended their plotting. KSM, alone, was working on multiple plots when he was captured.

Here's an example of how the interrogation program actually worked to disrupt terrorist plotting. Without revealing to KSM that Hambali had been captured, we asked him who might take over in the event that Hambali was no longer around. KSM pointed to Hambali's brother Rusman Gunawan. We then found Gunawan, and information from him resulted in the takedown of a 17-member Southeast Asian cell that Gunawan had recruited for a "second wave," 9/11-style attack on the U.S. West Coast, in all likelihood using aircraft again to attack buildings. Had that attack occurred, the nightmare of 9/11 would have been repeated.

Enhanced Interrogation Can Produce Valuable Results

Robert Siegel and Peter Hoekstra

Robert Siegel is an American radio journalist. He has been one of the co-hosts of the National Public Radio evening news broadcast All Things Considered *since 1987. Peter "Pete" Hoekstra is a former member of the US House of Representatives, representing Michigan's second district. He was chair of the House Intelligence Committee from 2004–2007.*

Robert Siegel talks to Peter "Pete" Hoekstra, who was chair of the House Intelligence Committee from 2004-2007. He talks about the Senate Intelligence Committee's so-called torture report and talks about what he knew of the offenses at the time, and what he thinks of the report today.

ROBERT SIEGEL, HOST: Former Congressman Peter Hoekstra was chairman and later, Ranking Minority Member of the House Intelligence Committee. The Michigan Republican served nine terms in the House and he now works for a Washington law firm and at a Washington think tank.

Mr. Hoekstra, welcome to the program.

PETER HOEKSTRA: It's great to be with you. Thank you.

SIEGEL: You were a senior member of the committee that oversaw the CIA during the years described in the Senate report, the years after 9/11. First, do you share its general conclusions, number one that brutal interrogations produce little if any actionable intelligence?

HOEKSTRA: No, I don't agree with those conclusions at all. I think that in the mosaic of gathering intelligence, I personally believe that some of the intelligence that was received through the interrogation—the enhanced interrogation process—did help us more effectively combat the threat from radical jihadists.

SIEGEL: To take one major point though, one claim disputed by the Senate report is that those interrogation techniques produced information that led to Osama bin Laden. The report suggests that what was learned about bin Laden's courier— the main piece of intelligence—came from conventional interrogation methods.

Do you agree with the Agency or with the senators on that one?

HOEKSTRA: No, I agree with the Agency on this. I think in many ways the Agency's getting very much a bum rap by this Senate report. The business of intelligence is about connecting the dots and I'm firmly convinced that through the enhanced interrogation techniques, we collected dots that eventually helped us plan missions, including the raid on bin Laden that ultimately killed bin Laden, and so enhanced interrogations were part of that process to develop the full set of information that was necessary.

SIEGEL: Judging from your reaction to the report and what the CIA said in reaction to the release of the report, it sounds to me as though you would have no problem with the CIA still waterboarding terror suspects?

HOEKSTRA: That's an unfair characterization.

SIEGEL: Where do you find anything wrong with what's been done? You seem to have felt it was all justified.

HOEKSTRA: Well, no—I think—having had, or having a very fair discussion, a bipartisan discussion, as to exactly what enhanced interrogation techniques worked, how effective were they, what alternatives were available—I think that would be a very worthwhile and meaningful discussion to have. And I'm disappointed that this report that came out from the Senate was only endorsed by Senate Democrats and that it was not a bipartisan report, and that some of the people who were involved in this process were never even interviewed. And you know, there were parts of the thing—this process—that I disagreed with very strongly. When Jose Rodriguez destroyed tapes of waterboarding...

SIEGEL: He was the CIA counterterrorism...

HOEKSTRA: ...He was the CIA Counterterrorism Head. You know, and Congress—when we found out that those tapes were available, we requested access to those tapes and to view them, and the CIA destroyed them. I very much disagreed with that and I thought that Jose Rodriguez or whoever made that decision should be held accountable, either through proceedings by the Justice Department, or a reprimand by Congress.

SIEGEL: But just to be clear though, when the Agency says that its techniques led to bin Laden, among those, among the interrogations they're talking about, is the interrogation of Khalid Sheikh Mohammed and I believe Abu Zubaydah. They accounted for most of the waterboarding being done, so I'm not quite sure whether you're saying that is effective and it leads to actionable intelligence that helps to achieve important strategic goals, or whether it should be stopped—it should've been stopped.

HOEKSTRA: Well, what I can tell you is, at the time, when briefed on interrogation techniques and shown or verbally described exactly how those techniques would be used, where they would be used and their effectiveness in the past, the Republican and

Democratic leadership in the House on intelligence all agreed that those should continue to be viable options for our intelligence community to use, depending on the circumstances and depending on the individual that may have been apprehended.

SIEGEL: Let me ask you a question about one word—torture. The Senate report describes the treatment of an Afghan man in his mid-50s named Arsala Khan who was believed to have helped bin Laden flee in 2001. Fifty-six hours of standing sleep deprivation, after which he's described by a—in a CIA document as barely able to enunciate and suffering hallucinations. Then two days of being allowed sleep, then 21 more hours of sleep deprivation. Eventually, freed and compensated. He was of no use, it turned out, as an intelligence source.

Would you say that he was tortured?

HOEKSTRA: I would say that, you know, there's a legal definition for that and the procedures and the techniques, you know and this is—yeah, hiding behind a legal description, but that the Justice Department and internal attorneys within the administration would have said that that was not torture.

SIEGEL: But I mean, in common English, would you say that man was tortured by his interrogators?

HOEKSTRA: I think reasonable people could say that that man was tortured but, you know, where we're getting into now is, we're —and you know, this is always the hard part of intelligence and these types of things, designing and determining exactly where you will cross the line and you move from enhanced interrogations into torture and different people will draw that line a different place.

Was I uncomfortable at some of the descriptions of some of the activities as they were outlined to me? Yes.

SIEGEL: Since you agree with the CIA's appraisal that indeed these techniques did produce actionable intelligence and they lead to very important goals, like getting Osama bin Laden, as the U.S. looks forward, to say, coping with ISIS in Iraq or Syria, or dealing with other groups that pose terror threats either to U.S. interests abroad or to the United States—should we restore these techniques? Should we say, you know, someone who's detained and might be linked to such a group should be potentially subjected to sleep deprivation, water boarding? Should we say, yeah, let's go back to what we were doing in the years right after 9/11?

HOEKSTRA: No, we should never go back and just do it. What we should do is a very common practice in the business community where I came, or the military or the intelligence community. We should do a lessons-learned. What we need today on foreign policy, what we need in the intelligence community is we need bipartisanship agreement. We have real threats that are out there. We need America to come together with strategies to confront these threats effectively for the long term, and a discussion—an informed discussion on the use and effectiveness of enhanced interrogation techniques is totally appropriate. And that should then frame where we move in the future.

SIEGEL: Peter Hoekstra, former Congressman Peter Hoekstra, former chairman of the House Intelligence Committee.

Thank you so much for talking with us today.

HOEKSTRA: Great. Thank you.

AUDIE CORNISH, HOST: Elsewhere in the program, a former military interrogator, he disputes the value of enhanced interrogations. He'll explain the different techniques he used to help get the information that led U.S. forces to the leader of al-Qaida in Iraq. Meanwhile, you can read excerpts from that Senate intelligence report and hear more interviews from many other players in this story at our website, npr.org.

The Enhanced Interrogation Program Failed

ThinkProgress

ThinkProgress is an American political news blog. It is a media project of the Center for American Progress (CAP), a progressive public policy research and advocacy organization.

I. TORTURE DOES NOT YIELD ACCURATE INTELLIGENCE
Military, Intelligence Experts: Info From Enhanced Techniques Is Unreliable

Gen. Petraeus: Torture yields information "of questionable value." "Some may argue that we would be more effective if we sanctioned torture or other expedient methods to obtain information from the enemy. That would be wrong. Beyond the basic fact that such actions are illegal, history shows that they also are frequently neither useful nor necessary. Certainly, extreme physical action can make someone 'talk;' however, what the individual says may be of questionable value." [Gen. David Petraeus, Letter to Multi-National Force-Iraq, 5/10/07]

FBI warns military interrogators: Enhanced techniques are "of questionable effectiveness." Defense Department interrogators "were being encouraged at times to use aggressive interrogation tactics in GTMO which are of questionable effectiveness and subject to uncertain interpretation based on law and regulation. Not only are these tactics at odds with legally permissible interviewing techniques used by U.S. law enforcement agencies in the United States, but they are being employed by personnel in GTMO who appear to have little, if any, experience eliciting information for judicial purposes. The continued use of these techniques has

"Why Bush's 'Enhanced Interrogation' Program Failed," ThinkProgress, May 5, 2009. Reprinted by permission.

the potential of negatively impacting future interviews by FBI agents as they attempt to gather intelligence and prepare cases for prosecution." [FBI memo, 5/30/03]

FBI cites "lack of evidence of [enhanced techniques'] success." "The differences between DHS and FBI interrogation techniques and the potential legal problems which could arise were discussed with DHS officials. However, they are adamant that their interrogation strategies are the best ones to use despite the lack of evidence of their success." [FBI memo, 5/30/03]

Army JAG: "I don't think [torture] is all that effective." "If you torture somebody, they'll tell you anything. I don't know anybody that is good at interrogation, has done it a lot, that will say that that's an effective means of getting information. ... So I don't think it's effective." [Major General Thomas Romig, former Army JAG, 11/19/07]

Special Ops Interrogator: "Enhanced" interrogation causes detainees to "shut up." "When I was in Iraq, the few times that I saw people use harsh methods, it was always counterproductive. Because the person hunkered down, they were expecting us to do that, and they just shut up. And then I'd have to send somebody in and build back up rapport, reverse that process, and it'd take us longer to get that information." [Matthew Alexander, leader of a Special Operations interrogation team in Iraq, 12/8/08]

FBI Special Agent Jack Cloonan: Rapport-building method yields better results. "It is my belief, based on a 27 year career as a Special Agent and interviews with hundreds of subjects in custodial settings, including members of al Qaeda, that the use of coercive interrogation techniques is not effective. The alternative approach, sometimes referred to as 'rapport building' is more effective, efficient and reliable. Scientists, psychiatrists, psychologists, law enforcement and intelligence agents, all of whom have studied both approaches, have came to the same conclusion. The CIA's own training manual advises its agents that heavy-handed techniques can impair a subject's ability to accurately recall information and, at worst, produce apathy and complete withdrawal." [FBI special agent Jack Cloonan, testimony to Congress 6/10/08]

Military's Joint Personnel Recovery Agency [JPRA] cautioned enhanced program produces unreliable intelligence. "The [Dec. 2001] memo [to the Department of Defense General Counsel] cautioned, however, that while '[p]hyisical deprivations can and do work in altering the prisoners' mental state to the point where they will say things they normally would not say,' use of physical deprivations has "several major downfalls.' JPRA warned that physical deprivations were 'not as effective' a means of getting information as psychological pressures, that information gained from their use was 'less reliable,' and that their use 'tends to increase resistance postures when deprivations are removed.'" [Senate Armed Services Report on Detainee Treatment and Abuse, Nov. 2008, p.38]

Army Intelligence Officer Col. Herrington: Enhanced techniques endanger intelligence collection. "COL Herrington also warned that certain security procedures in place at the time could have a negative impact on intelligence collection, stating: 'The austere nature of the facilities and the rigorous security movement procedures (shackles, two MPs with hands on the detainee, etc.) reinforces to detainees that they are in prison, and detracts from the flexibility that debriefers require to accomplish their mission… These views have nothing to do with being "soft" on the detainees. Nor do they challenge the pure security gains from such tight control. The principal at work is that optimal exploitation of a detainee cannot be done from a cell.'" [Senate Armed Services Report on Detainee Treatment and Abuse, Nov. 2008, p.44]

Army psychologist: Enhanced techniques "do not work" in intelligence-gathering. "It was stressed to me time and time again that psychological investigations have proven that harsh interrogations do not work. At best it will get you information that a prisoner thinks you want to hear to make the interrogation stop, but that information is strongly likely to be false." [MAJ Paul Burney, Army's Behavior Science Consulting Team psychologist, statement to Committee, 8/21/07. Senate Armed Services Report, p.78]

Army psychologist: Rapport techniques produce better intelligence. "Experts in the field of interrogation indicate the most effective interrogation strategy is a rapport-building approach. Interrogation techniques that rely on physical or adverse consequences are likely to garner inaccurate information and create an increased level of resistance…There is no evidence that the level of fear or discomfort evoked by a given technique has any consistent correlation to the volume or quality of information obtained." [Maj. Burney, BSCT Psychiatrist, Oct. 2002 memo to JTF-170. Senate Armed Services Report, p.83]

FBI to Gitmo Commander: Gitmo techniques are "highly skeptical." "Many of [JTF-GTMO's] methods are considered coercive by Federal Law Enforcement and UCMJ standards. Not only this, but reports from those knowledgeable about the use of these coercive techniques are highly skeptical as to their effectiveness and reliability." [Nov. 22, 2002 memo to MG Geoffrey Miller, who commanded JTF Gitmo. Senate Armed Services Report, p.115]

SERE specialist: Stress positions "are not effective" for gaining intelligence. "According to his testimony, 'history has shown us that physical pressures are not effective for compelling an individual to give information or to do something' and are not effective for gaining accurate, actionable intelligence." [Terrence Russell, JPRA's manager for research and development and a SERE specialist, testimony to Committee, 8/3/07. Senate Armed Services Report, p.209]

FBI Director Robert Meuller: Enhanced techniques haven't prevented any attacks. "So far as he is aware, have any attacks on America been disrupted thanks to intelligence obtained through what the administration still calls 'enhanced techniques'? 'I'm really reluctant to answer that,' Mueller says. He pauses, looks at an aide, and then says quietly, declining to elaborate: 'I don't believe that has been the case.'" [Vanity Fair, 12/16/08]

Former CIA Interrogator: Information from torture is unreliable. "[Coercive techniques] didn't provide useful, meaningful, trustworthy information…Everyone was deeply concerned and most felt it was un-American and did not work." [Glenn L. Carle, a retired C.I.A. officer who oversaw the interrogation of a high-level detainee in 2002, New York Times, 5/03/11]

The Interrogations Of Zubaydah And KSM: Enhanced Techniques Produced No Actionable Intelligence
FBI's Jack Cloonan: Zubaydah and KSM gave only "pabulum." "The proponents of torture say, 'Look at the body of information that has been obtained by these methods.' But if K.S.M. and Abu Zubaydah did give up stuff, we would have heard the details," says FBI agent Jack Cloonan. "What we got was pabulum." [Vanity Fair, 12/16/08]

CIA Official: CIA interrogations of KSM produced "total f*cking bullsh*t." "But according to a former senior C.I.A. official, who read all the interrogation reports on K.S.M., '90 percent of it was total f*cking bullsh*t.' A former Pentagon analyst adds: 'K.S.M. produced no actionable intelligence. He was trying to tell us how stupid we were.'" [Vanity Fair, 12/16/08]

FBI Interrogator Ali Soufan: Torturing Zubaydah was unnecessary. "I've kept my mouth shut about all this for seven years," Soufan says. But now, with the declassification of Justice memos and the public assertions by Cheney and others that "enhanced" techniques worked, Soufan feels compelled to speak out. "I was in the middle of this, and it's not true that these [aggressive] techniques were effective," he says. "We were able to get the information about Khalid Sheikh Mohammed in a couple of days. We didn't have to do any of this [torture]. We could have done this the right way." [Newsweek, 5/4/09]

Zubaydah revealed KSM's Identity BEFORE being tortured. "He [Zubaydah] was transferred from Pakistan to Thailand, where Soufan and Gaudin immediately sought to gain his trust by nursing his wounds. … During this time, Soufan and Gaudin also began the questioning; it became a 'mental poker game.' At first, Abu Zubaydah even denied his identity, insisting that his name was 'Daoud.' But Soufan had poured through the bureau's intelligence files and stunned Abu Zubaydah when he called him 'Hani'—the nickname that his mother used for him. Soufan also showed him photos of a number of terror suspects who were high on the bureau's priority list. Abu Zubaydah looked at one of them and said, 'That's Mukhtar.' Now it was Soufan who was stunned. The FBI had been trying to determine the identity of a mysterious 'Mukhtar,' whom bin Laden kept referring to on a tape he made after 9/11. Now Soufan knew: Mukhtar was the man in the photo, terror fugitive Khalid Sheikh Mohammed, and, as Abu Zubaydah blurted out, 'the one behind 9/11.' … Soon enough, Abu Zubaydah offered up more information—about the bizarre plans of a jihadist from Puerto Rico to set off a 'dirty bomb' inside the country. This information led to Padilla's arrest in Chicago by the FBI in early May." [Newsweek, 5/4/09]

CIA enhanced techniques "changed the tenor" of Zubaydah's interrogation. "But the tenor of the Abu Zubaydah interrogations changed a few days later, when a CIA contractor showed up. Although Soufan declined to identify the contractor by name, other sources (and media accounts) identify him as James Mitchell, a former Air Force psychologist who had worked on the U.S. military's Survival, Evasion, Resistance and Escape training—a program to teach officers how to resist the abusive interrogation methods used by Chinese communists during the Korean War. Within days of his arrival, Mitchell—an architect of the CIA interrogation program—took charge of the questioning of Abu Zubaydah. He directed that Abu Zubaydah be ordered to answer questions or face a gradual increase in aggressive techniques. One day Soufan entered Abu Zubadyah's room and saw that he had been stripped naked; he covered him with a towel." [Newsweek, 5/4/09]

FBI's Soufan: CIA's "enhanced interrogation" destroyed progress with Zubaydah; traditional methods provided "important actionable intelligence." "Abu Zubaydah was making progress before torture techniques. One of the most striking parts of the memos is the false premises on which they are based. The first, dated August 2002, grants authorization to use harsh interrogation techniques on a high-ranking terrorist, Abu Zubaydah, on the grounds that previous methods hadn't been working. The next three memos cite the successes of those methods as a justification for their continued use. It is inaccurate, however, to say that Abu Zubaydah had been uncooperative. Along with another F.B.I. agent, and with several C.I.A. officers present, I questioned him from March to June 2002, before the harsh techniques were introduced later in August. Under traditional interrogation methods, he provided us with important actionable intelligence." [Ali Soufan, New York Times op-ed, 4/23/09]

Soufan: Enhanced techniques on Zubaydah produced "no actionable intelligence." "Nothing gained from torture of Abu Zubaydah produced information that wouldn't have come from traditional techniques. We discovered, for example, that Khalid

Shaikh Mohammed was the mastermind of the 9/11 attacks. Abu Zubaydah also told us about Jose Padilla, the so-called dirty bomber. This experience fit what I had found throughout my counterterrorism career: traditional interrogation techniques are successful in identifying operatives, uncovering plots and saving lives. There was no actionable intelligence gained from using enhanced interrogation techniques on Abu Zubaydah that wasn't, or couldn't have been, gained from regular tactics." [Ali Soufan, New York Times op-ed, 4/23/09]

Soufan: Padilla, KSM, other plots disclosed through regular interrogation, NOT torture. "Claims that torture led to disclosure of Khalid Shaikh Mohammad is false. Defenders of these techniques have claimed that they got Abu Zubaydah to give up information leading to the capture of Ramzi bin al-Shibh, a top aide to Khalid Shaikh Mohammed, and Mr. Padilla. This is false. The information that led to Mr. Shibh's capture came primarily from a different terrorist operative who was interviewed using traditional methods. As for Mr. Padilla, the dates just don't add up: the harsh techniques were approved in the memo of August 2002, Mr. Padilla had been arrested that May." [Ali Soufan, New York Times op-ed, 4/23/09]

Zubaydah made false confessions after enhanced interrogation. "The tribunal president, a colonel whose name is redacted, asked him: 'So I understand that during this treatment, you said things to make them stop and then those statements were actually untrue, is that correct?' Abu Zubaydah replied: 'Yes.'" [Vanity Fair, 12/16/08]

Enhanced Interrogations Led To False
Claims Of Iraq/Al Qaeda Link
Enhanced techniques led to false Iraq/AQ link claims. "There was much more, says the analyst who worked at the Pentagon: 'I first saw the reports soon after Abu Zubaydah's capture. There was a lot of stuff about the nuts and bolts of al-Qaeda's supposed relationship with the Iraqi Intelligence Service. The intelligence

community was lapping this up, and so was the administration, obviously. Abu Zubaydah was saying Iraq and al-Qaeda had an operational relationship. It was everything the administration hoped it would be.'" [Vanity Fair, 12/16/08]

Interrogators resorted to "enhanced techniques" after "pressure" to find Iraq/Al Qaeda link. "'While we were there [at Guantanamo] a large part of the time we were focused on trying to establish a link between al Qaida and Iraq and we were not successful in establishing a link between al Qaida and Iraq,' [BCST psychologist Maj. Paul] Burney told staff of the Army Inspector General. 'The more frustrated people got in not being able to establish that link . . . there was more and more pressure to resort to measures that might produce more immediate results.'" [McClatchy on Senate Armed Services Report, 4/21/09]

II. TORTURE MAKES AMERICANS LESS SAFE

Enhanced Interrogations Recruits Terrorists

FBI's Jack Cloonan: 'Revenge in the form of a catastrophic attack' is possible. "Based on my experience in talking to Al Qaida members, I am persuaded that revenge in the form of a catastrophic attack on the homeland is coming; that a new generation of jihadist martyrs, motivated in part by the images from Abu Ghraib, is, as we speak, planning to kill Americans; and that nothing gleaned from the use of coercive interrogation techniques will be of any significant use in forestalling this calamitous eventuality." [FBI special agent Jack Cloonan, testimony to Congress, 6/10/08]

Sen. McCain: Torture is al Qaeda's best recruitment tool. "And most importantly, it serves as a great propaganda tool for those who recruit people to fight against us. And I've seen concrete examples of that talking to former high-ranking al-Qaeda individuals in Iraq." [Sen. John McCain (R-AZ) on Fox News, 4/20/09]

Adm. Mike Mullen: Torture is a recruiting symbol. "Well, the concern I've had about Guantanamo in these wars is it has been a symbol, and one which has been a recruiting symbol for those extremists and jihadists who would fight us." [Joint Chiefs of Staff Chairman Adm. Mike Mullen, ABC's This Week 5/24/09]

Special Ops Interrogator: Use of torture inspired anti-American fighters to Iraq. "I learned in Iraq that the No. 1 reason foreign fighters flocked there to fight were the abuses carried out at Abu Ghraib and Guantanamo. Our policy of torture was directly and swiftly recruiting fighters for al-Qaeda in Iraq." [Matthew Alexander, leader of a Special Operations interrogation team in Iraq, 11/30/08]

Colin Powell: Remove the recruitment incentive. "I think we ought to remove this incentive that exists in the presence of Guantanamo to encourage people and to give radicals an opportunity to say, you see, this is what America is all about. They're all about torture and detention centers." [Ret. Gen. Colin Powell, former Joint Chiefs Chairman and Secretary of State, 2/21/10]

Enhanced Interrogations Puts American Soldiers At Risk
Special Operations interrogator: Torture policies "directly and swiftly recruiting" al Qaeda fighters. "I learned in Iraq that the No. 1 reason foreign fighters flocked there to fight were the abuses carried out at Abu Ghraib and Guantanamo. Our policy of torture was directly and swiftly recruiting fighters for al-Qaeda in Iraq. ... It's no exaggeration to say that at least half of our losses and casualties in that country have come at the hands of foreigners who joined the fray because of our program of detainee abuse. The number of U.S. soldiers who have died because of our torture policy will never be definitively known, but it is fair to say that it is close to the number of lives lost on Sept. 11, 2001. How anyone can say that torture keeps Americans safe is beyond me—unless you don't count American soldiers as Americans." [Matthew Alexander, Washington Post op-ed, 11/30/08]

Army JAG: Enhanced techniques "has not made it safer" for captured U.S. soldiers. "I don't know how you could say we're safer and more secure. If you torture somebody, they'll tell you anything. I don't know anybody that is good at interrogation, has done it a lot, that will say that that's an effective means of getting information. … So I don't think it's effective. To that extent I don't see how it's made it safer. It has not made it safer for our soldiers when they're captured." [Major General Thomas Romig, former Army JAG, 11/19/07]

Navy general counsel: Torture is 1st and 2nd cause of death for U.S. troops. "[T]here are serving U.S. flag-rank officers who maintain that the first and second identifiable causes of U.S. combat deaths in Iraq—as judged by their effectiveness in recruiting insurgent fighters into combat—are, respectively the symbols of Abu Ghraib and Guantanamo." [Former Navy general counsel Aberto Mora, testimony to Congress, 6/17/08]

JAGs: Enhanced techniques endangers U.S. soldiers. "Employment of exception techniques may have a negative effect on the treatment of U.S. POWs by their captors and raises questions about the ability of the U.S. to call others to account for mistreatment of U.S. servicemembers." [memos from Deputy JAG of Air Force Jack Rives, Navy JAG Michael Lohr, and Staff JAG to the Commandant of the Marine Corps Kevin Sandkuhler, to Air Force General Counsel Mary Walker, Feb. 2003. Senate Armed Services Report, p.158]

Joint Forces Command JAG: Enhanced techniques threatens soldiers in the field. "I fail to see how anyone can reasonably say that employing such techniques against those in our custody is worthy of the United States, no matter how much we may need the information. In my view, for the U.S. to do this 'lowers the bar' and ensures, if there is any doubt, that similar techniques will be employed against any US personnel captured by our enemies." [E-mail from Capt. Daniel Donavan JFCOM (Joint Forces

Command) Staff Judge Advocate, to ADM Giambastiani, LTG Wagner, and Maj Gen Soligan, 5/13/04. Senate Armed Services Report, p.258]

Sen. John McCain (R-AZ): Torture increases danger to U.S. troops. "While our intelligence personnel in Abu Ghraib may have believed that they were protecting U.S. lives by roughing up detainees to extract information, they have had the opposite effect. Their actions have increased the danger to American soldiers, in this conflict and in future wars." [Sen. John McCain (R-AZ), Foreign Affairs, 6/01/04]

Enhanced Interrogations Ruin Credibility
Of Intelligence Agencies
Torture rebuilt "Chinese wall" between FBI and CIA, making Americans less safe. FBI's Ali Soufan: "Torture techniques hinders intelligence by driving wedge deeper between CIA and FBI. One of the worst consequences of the use of these harsh techniques was that it reintroduced the so-called Chinese wall between the C.I.A. and F.B.I., similar to the communications obstacles that prevented us from working together to stop the 9/11 attacks. Because the bureau would not employ these problematic techniques, our agents who knew the most about the terrorists could have no part in the investigation. An F.B.I. colleague of mine who knew more about Khalid Shaikh Mohammed than anyone in the government was not allowed to speak to him." [Ali Soufan, New York Times op-ed, 4/23/09]

Enhanced interrogation destroys reputation of CIA, making Americans less safe. "Not only are torture methods ineffective, they harm future effectiveness of any techniques because they harm US reputation. As we move forward, it's important to not allow the torture issue to harm the reputation, and thus the effectiveness, of the C.I.A. The agency is essential to our national security." [Ali Soufan, New York Times op-ed, 4/23/09]

Enhanced techniques program created wedge between military officials and Bush administration/CIA. The policy was anathema to military people, starting with Colin Powell, a retired general and secretary of state in the first Bush term. Says Mr. Mora [Alberto Mora, general counsel of the U.S. Navy in 2001]: "I never met a senior military officer that didn't object to these policies. They caused the senior military to hold the Bush administration in contempt." [New York Times, 5/3/09]

Bad intelligence wastes FBI's time following false leads. "At the F.B.I., says a seasoned counterterrorist agent, following false leads generated through torture has caused waste and exhaustion. 'At least 30 percent of the F.B.I.'s time, maybe 50 percent, in counterterrorism has been spent chasing leads that were bullshit. There are "lead squads" in every office trying to filter them. But that's ineffective, because there's always that "What if?" syndrome." [Vanity Fair, 12/16/08]

Enhanced Interrogations Strain Alliances
Enhanced tactics strain alliances and threatens intelligence-sharing. "There is another variable in the intelligence equation: the help you lose because your friends start keeping their distance. When I worked at the State Department, some of America's best European allies found it increasingly difficult to assist us in counterterrorism because they feared becoming complicit in a program their governments abhorred. This was not a hypothetical concern." [Philip Zelikow, former deputy to Secretary of State Condoleezza Rice, New York Times op-ed, 4/24/09]

FBI: Torture makes allies less willing to work with us. "Torture degrades our image abroad and complicates our working relationships with foreign law enforcement and intelligence agencies." [FBI special agent Jack Cloonan, testimony to Congress 6/10/08]

Air Force Colonel: U.S. lacks credibility abroad because of torture. "[T]he lack of expertise at the senior level in managing and conducting interrogation was a single point of failure that facilitated introduction of SERE techniques into the repertoire of allowable interrogation methods. As a result, adversaries and allies alike have accused this nation of gross violations of the Geneva Convention and of violating the basic human rights of those in detention. The geostrategic consequences are likely to last decades." [Colonel Steven M. Kleinman, USAFR, Former Director of Intelligence Personnel Recovery Academy, Joint Personnel Recovery Agency, Senate testimony, 9/25/08]

Interrogations Ruined America's Moral Authority

Gen. Petraeus: U.S. must occupy 'the moral high ground.' "Adherence to our values distinguishes us from our enemy. This fight depends on securing the population, which must understand that we—not our enemies—occupy the moral high ground." [Gen. David Petraeus, Letter to Multi-National Force-Iraq, 5/10/07]

Military Intelligence Officer: "We need to…remember who we are." "As for 'the gloves need to come off…' we need to take a deep breath and remember who we are. Those gloves are most definitely NOT based on Cold War or WWII enemies—they are based on clearly established standards of international law to which we are signatories and in part the originators. Those in turn derive from practices commonly accepted as morally correct, the so-called 'usages of war.' It comes down to standards of right and wrong—something we cannot just put aside when we find it inconvenient…BOTTOM LINE: We are American soldiers, heirs to a long tradition of staying on the high ground. We need to stay there." [Maj. Nathan Hoepner, Operations Officer of 501st MI Battalion e-mail, 8/14/03. Senate Armed Services Report, p.200]

Army JAG: U.S. has always set the moral standard. "The United States had always taken the high road and set the standard internationally on treatment. There had never been any doubt. We had always set the standard. And now the danger is there's going to be a perception that, 'Well, the United States doesn't live to that standard—why should we?'" [Major General Thomas Romig, former Army JAG, 11/19/07]

Colin Powell: Torture has made people "question whether we're following our own high standards." "If you just look at how we are perceived in the world and the kind of criticism we have taken over Guantanamo, Abu Ghraib and renditions…whether we believe it or not, people are now starting to question whether we're following our own high standards." [Washington Post, 9/17/06]

America's negative reputation "strengthens the hand of our enemies." "The fact that America is seen in a negative light by so many complicates our ability to attract allies to our side, strengthens the hand of our enemies, and reduces our ability to collect intelligence that can save lives." [Conclusion of Senate Armed Services Report, p.27]

Former U.S. Navy General Counsel: Torture violates our founding values. "[O]ur Nation's policy decision to use so-called 'harsh interrogation techniques' during the war on terror was a mistake of massive proportions. It damaged, and continues to damage, our Nation. This policy, which may aptly be labeled a policy of cruelty, violated our founding values, our constitutional system, and the fabric of our laws, our overarching foreign policy interests, and our National security. The net effect of this policy of cruelty has been to weaken our defenses, not to strengthen them. All of these factors contributed to the difficulties our Nation has experienced in forging the strongest possible coalition to fight the war, but the damage to our National security also occurred down at the tactical or operational level." [Alberto Mora, Former General Counsel, United States Navy, Senate testimony, 6/17/08]

Enhanced Interrogations Makes Terrorists Unprosecutable
Bush official forced to suspect suspect's trial after deeming he was tortured. "We tortured [Mohammed al-]Qahtani," said Susan J. Crawford, in her first interview since being named convening authority of military commissions by Defense Secretary Robert M. Gates in February 2007. "His treatment met the legal definition of torture. And that's why I did not refer the case" for prosecution. [Washington Post, 1/14/09]

Enhanced interrogations make Guantanamo detainees ineligible for prosecution. The fear that some Guantanamo cases are not prosecutable in federal court has sharpened debate within the Obama administration about the need to maintain military commissions, in which the rules of evidence are less stringent, according to sources involved in the discussions. ... Responding to complaints from military groups that Marri's sentence is too short, a Justice Department spokesman said the possible 15-year term was the best deal the government could strike, given concerns about the release of classified evidence and the impact of possible testimony regarding Marri's mental state after prolonged solitary confinement. [Washington Post, 5/4/09]

III. HISTORICAL LESSONS CAUTION AGAINST ENHANCED TECHNIQUES

Enhanced Techniques Derived From
Ineffective Communist Tactics
Enhanced techniques taken from Communists' methods that had "wrung false confessions" from Americans. "According to several former top officials involved in the discussions seven years ago, they did not know that the military training program, called SERE, for Survival, Evasion, Resistance and Escape, had

been created decades earlier to give American pilots and soldiers a sample of the torture methods used by Communists in the Korean War, methods that had wrung false confessions from Americans. ... They did not know that some veteran trainers from the SERE program itself had warned in internal memorandums that, morality aside, the methods were ineffective." [New York Times, 4/21/09]

1950s study concluded techniques made prisoners "malleable and suggestible." "A little research on the origin of those methods would have given reason for doubt. Government studies in the 1950s found that Chinese Communist interrogators had produced false confessions from captured American pilots not with some kind of sinister 'brainwashing' but with crude tactics: shackling the Americans to force them to stand for hours, keeping them in cold cells, disrupting their sleep and limiting access to food and hygiene. ... Worse, the study found that under such abusive treatment, a prisoner became 'malleable and suggestible, and in some instances he may confabulate.'" [New York Times, 4/21/09]

Whole purpose of SERE training was to resist Communist tactics. "Using those techniques for interrogating detainees was also inconsistent with the goal of collecting accurate intelligence information, as the purpose of SERE resistance training is to increase the ability of U.S. personnel to resist abusive interrogations and the techniques were based, in part, on Chinese Communist techniques used during the Korean War to elicit false confessions." [Senate Armed Services Report, p.28]

British understood that physical violence was "unintelligent" and useless in gaining information. "[Colonel Robin 'Tin Eye'] Stephens [commander of Camp 020, the British spy prison] did not eschew torture out of mercy. This was no squishy liberal: the eye was made of tin, and the rest of him out of tungsten. (Indeed, he was disappointed that only 16 spies were executed during the war.) His motives were strictly practical. 'Never strike a man. It is unintelligent, for the spy will give an answer to please, an answer to escape punishment. And having given a false answer, all else depends upon the false premise.'" ["The Truth that Tin Eye saw," Times of London, 2/10/06]

Enhanced Interrogation Methods Have Not Been Proven to Incite Cooperation

Ken Klippenstein and Joseph Hickman

Ken Klippenstein is a freelance American journalist based in Madison, Wisconsin. He often writes about international affairs.

Joseph Hickman is a former US Marine and Army sergeant. He is the author of The Convenient Terrorist: Two Whistleblowers' Stories of Torture, Terror, Secret Wars, and CIA Lies.

It is early on in Abu Zubaydah's time at a CIA black site. He insists to his interrogators that he has no additional information on jihadist operations planned against the US, but his captor won't stop slapping him. Eventually a hood is placed over Zubaydah's head and he is placed into a confinement box by unseen security officers. He is told this is his new home until he's prepared to provide information on operations against the US.

Several physically stressful hours in the confinement box fail to elicit any intelligence, so Zubaydah's captors place him in an even smaller box. He makes painful groans and is forced to scoot out of the box on his hindquarters when he's finally allowed out. He is immediately made to stand and backed up against a wall. Two interrogators begin to double-team him with rapid-fire questions. Zubaydah is told that if he does not cooperate, he will only bring more misery on himself. Again he denies having any additional knowledge, but this time, he isn't slapped. Instead, Zubaydah is hooded and a water board is brought into the cell.

Zubaydah is the first post-9/11 detainee to be waterboarded, and this is his first session. He coughs and vomits. The waterboarding

"CIA Documents Expose the Failed Torture Methods Used on Guantanamo's Most Famous Detainee," by Ken Klippenstein and Joseph Hickman, Ken Klippenstein, May 15, 2017. Reprinted by permission.

lasts for over two hours, but he still insists he does not have any additional information beyond that which he already provided to the FBI. He is then put into the larger confinement box, where he spends the rest of the evening. The interrogation process resumes in the morning: more slapping, zero new information, and more time in the smaller box.

This was a summary of CIA documents obtained by AlterNet's Grayzone Project. The records were originally obtained by Zubaydah's defense team through the discovery process and were provided to me by a source familiar with the case who considered their publication critical to the public's understanding of Zubaydah's treatment. The vast majority of the documents have not been available to the public prior to this story.

As clinically detailed as they are gut-wrenching, the documents comprise hundreds of pages on the interrogation of Zubaydah, perhaps Guantanamo Bay's most famous detainee. The files revealed here have renewed significance as Zubaydah has decided to testify about conditions at Guantanamo Bay despite the likelihood that it will imperil his legal situation.

The records also highlight the methods of psychologist James Mitchell, a top architect of the CIA's "enhanced interrogation program." Though Mitchell had previously worked as an Air Force psychologist, the Senate "Torture Report" noted that he had no prior experience as an interrogator. Mitchell's private contracting company had received over $80 million from the CIA by the time their contract was terminated in 2009. The contract was terminated because, as the CIA Inspector General put it, there was no reason to believe Mitchell's interrogation techniques were effective or even safe.

Mitchell and the US government originally believed Zubaydah to be a top leader of Al Qaeda who had knowledge of imminent plots against the US; however, the government would later concede that Zubaydah was never an Al Qaeda leader but still contend that he poses a threat. According to the US government, Zubaydah "possibly" knew in advance about the bombing of the USS *Cole* in 2000 and attacks on American embassies in Africa in 1998.

After his capture in Pakistan in 2002, Zubaydah was held in CIA black sites for four years where he was subjected to extended torture so intense he lost his left eye. Following his first waterboarding, he was subjected to the same form of torture 82 times. It is unclear the brutal methods applied to Zubaydah's body elicited any valuable intelligence.

Sadistic Torture Without Government Authorization

The CIA documents depict a cooperative Zubaydah who maintains throughout that he has no more information beyond what he shared initially with the FBI. The documents make frequent reference to his captors' desire to induce a sense of hopelessness that would force him to talk. Mitchell tries to instill despair not just through overt methods like waterboarding and constricting Zubaydah's movement within small boxes, but also through subtle tactics focused on disorientation and isolation from human contact.

In one instance, Mitchell's attempts to enhance Zubaydah's sense of isolation went well beyond the weeks he spent in solitary confinement. The documents describe Mitchell's plans to minimize even the human contact afforded by visits from medical staff, who were required to wear uniforms of solid color, conceal their facial features and skin and wear tinted goggles. The medical staff were required to use hand signals to deprive Zubaydah of hearing human speech. The security team followed the same procedures but instead wore solid black uniforms.

The disorientation process was no less thorough: the documents describe Mitchell's plans to put Zubaydah in a state of "pharmaceutical unconsciousness" whenever he was transported, even on a visit to the hospital. Mitchell required natural light be strictly prohibited in favor of bright lights, along with an all-white, colorless environment. The documents frequently describe a constant white noise intentionally produced, even during harsher methods like waterboarding. Finally, Mitchell scrupulously ensured that everything Zubaydah experienced—interrogations, medical care, etc.—was completely unpredictable, forming no predictable schedule.

Among the most shocking revelations in the files is the fact that the CIA engaged in torture even before it received legal authorization from the Bush administration's infamous "Torture Memos," which were signed on Aug. 1, 2002. For example, one document dated April 24, 2002—over three months before the CIA would receive authorization to employ "enhanced interrogation" techniques—describes Zubaydah's being subjected to 76-hour periods of deprivation and a stereo playing "loud rock music to enhance his sense of hopelessness." The document also notes the authorization for the use of a "confinement box" on Zubaydah.

Another document dated May 2002 notes, "AZ [Abu Zubaydah] has shown an exploitable vulnerability when it comes to the issue of his family. He became visibly disturbed when told we would show a picture of him to his mother…as he has indicated a concern for his family and all family related matters, this angle may prove effective in gaining the required leverage."

Another document predating the Torture Memos, dated July 2002, notes that the CIA had already had Zubaydah in solitary confinement for 30 consecutive days.

Although the CIA didn't receive authorization to engage in torture until August, the Bush administration had already been discussing it months prior; the Agency may have sensed which way the political winds were blowing and behaved in anticipation of formal authorization.

Torture Trials for the CIA?

AlterNet contacted interrogation expert Mark Fallon, an international security consultant who spent over 30 years as a special agent with the Naval Criminal Investigative Service and author of a new book detailing how the intelligence community enacted the torture program under the Bush administration. Fallon said prolonged sleep deprivation constitutes torture under the United Nations Convention Against Torture. Regarding its efficacy, Fallen stated that sleep deprivation "is counterproductive, if the aim is obtaining accurate and reliable information. The effects on a person's cognitive capabilities is diminished and memory is corrupted."

Fallon also said confinement boxes "absolutely" constitute torture, even under controlled and calculated conditions. He noted that from the perspective of an unknowing victim, confinement boxes could be mistaken for an execution. Regarding prolonged isolation, Fallon said, "From an interrogation professional perspective, tactics [like isolation] that produce dread are not considered effective methods in eliciting cooperation and could harden resistance."

Asked if the fact that these torture practices predated legal authorization could open the CIA up to prosecution, Fallon said, "Depending on where it occurred, it could already expose them to potential international trials, who don't recognize the dubious legal cover they received."

One document dated May 2002 addresses this question of legality, conceding that their interrogation techniques "do not always comport with traditional interrogation methods." Furthermore, the document expresses a belief that Zubaydah "is not entitled to the legal protections of the Geneva conventions."

CIA torture has newfound relevance in light of Donald Trump's flippant pro-torture rhetoric. In January, Trump said he believed waterboarding "does work" and that it is "foolish and so naïve" not to be allowed to waterboard. In February, Trump's language appeared to solidify into action when he picked for CIA deputy director a CIA officer who ran a black site in Thailand where terror suspects were tortured.

The documents of Zubaydah's torture expose in clear detail the savage reality of what torture means. Whatever one thinks of Zubaydah and his activities prior to being captured, it is hard not to pity him as Mitchell describes in cold, clinical terms the sadistic methods he inflicts on his subject's body and mind.

Consider this excerpt from a transcript of interrogation sessions on Aug. 12, 2002:

> Today is day nine of the "aggressive interrogation" phase. Zubaydah is moved from his confinement box. A wound he had sustained is cleaned and he is given Ensure, a liquid meal replacement. He is returned to the confinement box.
>
> Over nine hours later, Zubaydah is again moved from his confinement box, is seated on the floor and hooded. After his wound is inspected, he is sent back to the confinement box.
>
> Three hours later, Zubaydah is once again moved from his confinement box. This time, security wheels in the water board. Zubaydah sways and loses his balance, then rights himself. The interrogators strap him into the water board. [Large segments of text are classified.]
>
> After at least one session of waterboarding, Zubaydah still denies knowing anything beyond what he'd revealed initially; but the interrogators insist he knows more than he's letting on. Zubaydah is waterboarded again. Afterwards he is released and put back into his confinement box.
>
> 27 minutes later, Zubaydah is taken out of the confinement box and seated on the floor, hooded. Two hours later, he is made to stand against the wall. After an hour, Zubaydah is again seated on the floor and shortly thereafter a water board is brought in. Once Zubaydah's hood is removed, he sees the water board and looks at his interrogators. He slowly walks toward the waterboard of his own accord, lays down and begins shaking. [Large segments of text are redacted.]
>
> About 30 minutes later, interrogators depart the room. Seconds later, Zubaydah begins vomiting. The interrogators rush back into the room, unstrap Zubaydah and place him in an upright position so he doesn't choke to death on his own vomit. Afterward he is hooded and led back into the confinement box.

President Trump Is Wrong About Torture: It Doesn't Work

Vanessa Schipani

Vanessa Schipani is a science journalist and philosopher of science. She has written and photographed for publications such as the American Scholar, *the* Scientist, EARTH, EuroScientist *and* BioScience.

Donald Trump said that "enhanced interrogation … works." But scientists have shown that the stress and pain induced by techniques like waterboarding can impair memory, and, therefore, inhibit a person from recalling information.

Enhanced interrogation can entail techniques such as slapping a person in the face, sleep deprivation, cramped confinement and waterboarding—the last of which involves reducing airflow with water to trigger the feeling of drowning.

This isn't the first time Trump, the Republican presidential nominee, has claimed enhanced interrogation works. Back in February, he said:

> Trump, Feb. 17: Torture works. OK, folks? You know, I have these guys—"Torture doesn't work!"—believe me, it works. And waterboarding is your minor form. Some people say it's not actually torture. Let's assume it is. But they asked me the question: What do you think of waterboarding? Absolutely fine. But we should go much stronger than waterboarding.

More recently in a July 27 press conference, Trump doubled down on his claim and said, "I am a person that believes in enhanced interrogation, yes. And by the way, it works."

But research in neuroscience and psychology suggests otherwise. In a 2009 *Trends in Cognitive Sciences* review paper, Shane O'Mara, a brain researcher at Trinity College Dublin in Ireland, wrote, "The

"Trump on Torture," by Vanessa Schipani, FactCheck.org, a project of the Annenberg Public Policy Center, July 28, 2016. Reprinted by permission.

use of [enhanced interrogation] techniques appears motivated by a folk psychology that is demonstrably incorrect."

What is that folk psychology? O'Mara describes it as "the idea that repeatedly inducing shock, stress, anxiety, disorientation and lack of control is more effective than are standard interrogatory techniques in making suspects reveal information."

It is also assumed that this information is "reliable and veridical, as suspects will be motivated to end the interrogation by revealing this information from long-term memory," O'Mara says. But this idea is "unsupported by scientific evidence," he adds.

O'Mara goes on to say that "[s]olid scientific evidence of how repeated and extreme stress and pain affect memory and executive functions (such as planning or forming intentions) suggests that these techniques are unlikely to do anything other than the opposite of that intended by coercive or 'enhanced' interrogation."

So what does the scientific literature say on the matter? In his review, O'Mara looked at research on how increased stress affects brain regions and mechanisms involved in memory function.

To start, while many brain functions remain elusive to neuroscientists and psychologists, memory formation and recall relies, in part, on a relatively well-understood mechanism—long-term synaptic potentiation, or LTP.

Scientists have investigated this mechanism through anatomical dissection and brain imaging, among other techniques, in both lab animals and humans since the 1970s. In particular, researchers have found that this mechanism is disrupted by extreme and prolonged stress and pain, explains O'Mara. Studies on rats and mice dating back to 1987 support this conclusion.

O'Mara also explains that the hippocampus and prefrontal cortices, regions of the brain, are both "essential for normal memory function." These regions of the brain are involved in LTP. When an individual is stressed, especially for long periods, these brain regions become compromised.

How? Stress causes the release of hormones like cortisol, which impair the function in these brain regions, sometimes even resulting in tissue loss, explains O'Mara. And when these regions are compromised, people have trouble recalling both short- and long-term memories. "[P]rolonged and sustained sleep deprivation, in part because it results in a substantial increase in cortisol levels, has a deleterious effect on memory," he says.

For example, in a 2009 paper published in *Nature Reviews Neuroscience*, which O'Mara cites, Amy F. T. Arnsten, an expert at Yale in both neuroscience and psychology, reviewed both human and animal studies that looked at the effect of stress on the prefrontal cortex.

Arnsten writes that studies have found, "Even quite mild acute uncontrollable stress can cause a rapid and dramatic loss of prefrontal cognitive abilities, and more prolonged stress exposure" can permanently change the structure of the region for the worse.

It may also be difficult to "determine during interrogation whether the information that a suspect reveals is true," argues O'Mara. Why? Information "presented by the captor to elicit responses during interrogation might inadvertently become part of the suspect's memory, especially because suspects are under extreme stress and are required to tell and retell the same events that might have happened over a period of years."

His argument relies on the science behind confabulation, or the production of false memories, as it's "a common consequence of frontal lobe disorders," explains O'Mara. And as already noted, prolonged and extreme stress has a negative effect on this brain region's function and structure. Thus, he says, "distinguishing between confabulations and what is true in the verbal statements of tortured suspects will be difficult."

O'Mara also cites studies that looked at the function of the frontal lobes in individuals with post traumatic stress disorder. "Brain imaging in people previously subjected to severe torture suggests that abnormal patterns of activation are present in the frontal and temporal lobes ... leading to deficits in verbal memory for the recall of traumatic events," O'Mara writes.

O'Mara concludes his paper stating that "coercive interrogations involving extreme stress are unlikely to facilitate the release of veridical information from long-term memory, given our current cognitive neurobiological knowledge." On the contrary, he adds, "these techniques cause severe, repeated and prolonged stress, which compromises brain tissue supporting memory and executive function."

To top it off, a report on the matter from the Senate Select Committee on Intelligence said: "The CIA's use of its enhanced interrogation techniques was not an effective means of acquiring intelligence or gaining cooperation from detainees." The report, released in 2014, adds, "The CIA's justification for the use of its enhanced interrogation techniques rested on inaccurate claims of their effectiveness."

In sum, while Trump says that enhanced interrogation "works," scientific evidence from neuroscience and psychology—and the Senate intelligence committee—says that it doesn't.

CHAPTER 2

Is Enhanced Interrogation Morally Defensible?

Overview: The Complex Moral Debate Over Enhanced Interrogation and Torture

Molly Guinness

Molly Guinness is based in Paris, where she works at Radio France Internationale. She has written for the Spectator, *the* Times Literary Supplement, *and* Literary Review.

This week's Senate Report on the CIA hasn't settled the question of torture once and for all, as Bruce Anderson has pointed out. When we talk about the heroes of the Resistance, our deepest admiration is reserved for the fighters who didn't give away their secrets under torture, so the claim that the CIA's enhanced interrogation techniques did not result in any useful intelligence is rather surprising: it's too morally neat.

British law has never condoned torture (though the Tudors found ways round that), and when the Italian philosopher Cesare Beccaria was trying to reform the European criminal justice system, Britain was already setting a good example:

> When Beccaria published his famous treatise On Crimes and Punishments in 1764, there were, it is said, only three European States in which prisoners and important witnesses at criminal trials were not examined under torture; they were England, Sweden and Prussia. Elsewhere the system was more or less taken for granted. It is the glory of Beccaria that he altered that state of mind, and caused to be recognised throughout Europe what had hitherto been little seen outside the three named countries, viz., that evidence wrung by torture is worthless, and that the process of wringing it is a monstrous wrong, since a large proportion of its victims must be innocent persons.

"Is Torture Acceptable If It Helps Save Thousands of Lives?" by Molly Guinness, The Spectator, December 14, 2014. Reprinted by permission.

These propositions may seem nearly self-evident. But they will always tend to be ignored by such servants of the State as are primarily concerned not to do justice but to secure convictions—a concern which used in many countries to be that of the judges, and must always and in any country remain, in varying degrees, that of the police.

There's a difference, though, between using torture to exact confessions and using it to get intelligence out of someone. Either way, it's a grim business. When he joined the army in 1949, Geoffrey Strickland found officers breezily recommending torture to young recruits and lecturing them on the best techniques:

> The purpose of the torture was solely to obtain valuable information from an enemy who treated British prisoners at the very least harshly. The methods employed were devised to inflict the maximum discomfort and pain while leaving as few as possible traces visible to the eyes of any visiting Red Cross official. One way was to force water down a prisoner's throat and strain the walls of his stomach, though this required considerable practice and skill. Another was to hold him near a hot stove. And one could simply beat him up, having first wrapped him in wet blankets, which would reduce the risk of externally visible bruises. There have been worse tortures obviously, but these seemed bad enough.

He spent the next few decades trying to draw attention to the story, but without much success. One academic told him the public conscience needed to preserve a certain innocence:

> If morality is the choice of a lesser evil, then torture itself may be morally unobjectionable, however grim the necessity and dangerous the precedent. Yet to condone torture on such occasions may amount in practice to condoning torture in general and even when its use is unnecessary or gratuitous. To say "No, some things are wrong in themselves, whatever their immediate consequences" may be justified in the long run, even on utilitarian grounds. Should the public, in any case, know what is being done in its name or was the eminent academic right about the public conscience? If the public knows, the knowledge

will either ensure that the practice is stopped which is fine if it ought to be stopped—or generate even greater secrecy on the part of those responsible and leave us more or less where we are now.

After the September 11th attacks, the priority was stopping another attack, but Paul Robinson argued that some of the methods employed went against everything we were fighting for:

> Already in this country we have David Blunkett with his plans for "pre-emptive detention," secret trials and the indefinite imprisonment of suspects on evidence which the Home Office has admitted might come from torture in other countries. The slippery slope from Blunkettism to state terrorism is but a short one, and if we do not start the fight against it now, we may find we have lost already.
>
> Despite Tony Blair's bizarre rantings, terrorism does not pose an "existential" threat to our society. Our civilisation is under threat, but not from terrorists, whose power is extremely limited. Only we ourselves can destroy the values that we cherish and which make us great. We must hold on to the principles that guarantee our superiority—our respect for the innocent, for due process and for justice. If we stand firm, we can never be defeated.

One of the people Robinson attacked was the lawyer Alan Dershowitz, who hit back with a letter in the next edition:

> Paul Robinson's purported description of my views on torture are a complete fabrication, as anyone actually reading my extensive body of writing on this subject can attest. I am against torture as a normative matter. As an empirical matter, however, I recognise that it is going on beneath the surface and under the radar screen. In order to bring this problem to the surface, so as to make those employing torture accountable, I have proposed that under no circumstances should torture ever be permitted without a judicial warrant. I do not "recommend" the insertion of sterilised needles under the fingernails. I simply used that as an illustration of the kind of non-lethal torture that might be considered under a torture warrant proposal.

Dershowitz didn't spark nearly as much controversy as John Yoo, who became known as Professor Torture after arguing that the president should be in charge of deciding how far interrogators could go when questioning suspects. Alasdair Palmer met him in 2007:

> Given his reputation, I was a little nervous about meeting John Yoo. I half-expected to encounter the kind of man who bites the head off a chicken each morning, and who has electrodes at the ready in his office. In reality… Prof. Yoo is gentle and reticent, and listens without interrupting. He's polite, courteous and not yet 40. He gives the impression of being a conscientious academic eager to find out what the law is and to ensure that it is never flouted.
>
> Flouting the law is, however, precisely what he stands accused of doing by writing the Torture Memo. "I reject that criticism totally," he says. "Everything I did was carefully crafted to make sure that it was consistent with the existing legislation. My obligation was to make sure that what the President did was lawful, and I took the obligation very seriously."

In the memo, he'd written that "acts must be of an extreme nature to rise to the level of torture… To amount to torture, an act must be equivalent in intensity to the pain accompanying serious physical injury, such as organ failure or even death." He gave examples of forms of treatment he did not think constituted torture, including kicking someone, forcing him to stand against a wall, subjecting him to noise and depriving him of sleep:

> It is all very specific, and very unpleasant. Even if he's right about what American law permits, wouldn't it just have been better left unsaid? "That was simply not an option," Yoo asserts. "The CIA wanted—needed—a definitive answer to the question: how far can we go? They had specifically requested a legal opinion. They had captured senior al-Qaeda operatives who were not responding to being asked questions politely. CIA officers needed to know what, legally, they were entitled to do to them to get them to talk. They knew these guys had information on what al-Qaeda was planning. If the CIA could get that information,

they could save lives. But they also wanted to be sure they would not end up going to prison for doing so."

"No question about it," he says. "Look, death is worse than torture, but everyone except pacifists thinks there are circumstances in which war is justified. War means killing people. If we are entitled to kill people, we must be entitled to injure them. I don't see how it can be reasonable to have an absolute prohibition on torture when you don't have an absolute prohibition on killing. Reasonable people will disagree about when torture is justified. But that, in some circumstances, it is justified seems to me to be just moral common sense. How could it be better that 10,000 or 50,000 or a million people die than that one person be injured?"

Alasdair Palmer had actually taken a similar line a couple of years earlier, arguing that our views on shoot-to-kill were inconsistent with our views on torture:

> While all torture is certainly horrible, not all of it has to be ordered by thugs or inflicted by sadists. One of the most effective techniques of interrogation is said to rely on sleep deprivation. Sleep deprivation is classified as a form of torture, which it is, and is prohibited under European law. It seems extraordinary that we are willing to shoot terrorist suspects in order to save lives, but not to deprive them of sleep.

He cites several examples of where torture has foiled terrorist plots, including an al-Qaeda plan in 1995 to crash 11 aeroplanes carrying 4,000 people into the Pacific. One US interrogator Chris Mackey (a pseudonym) wrote a book arguing that effective interrogation had become impossible as a result of the outright ban on torture under international law:

> Mackey notes that American soldiers managed to obtain an al-Qaeda manual on interrogation. That manual stated that "the Americans will not harm you physically" because "they are not warriors." The manual added that anyone captured by the Americans "must tempt them into striking you. And if they do strike you, you should complain to the authorities immediately...."

You could end an interrogator's career, and prompt a Red Cross investigation, if you could show a bruise or a scar." Chris Mackey reports that the most depressing thing for the US interrogators in Afghanistan at the time (2002) was the manual's accuracy. It was correct in its account of how al-Qa'eda members would be treated by the Americans. The truth was, as one of Mackey's co-interrogators commented, "You could lie to us, refuse to talk, switch your story from one session to the next, and there wasn't a damn thing we could do about it." There is no doubt that non-lethal torture techniques such as sleep deprivation, stress positions and hooding produce reliable information much more quickly and effectively than just asking politely.

In the war on terror, we will need those techniques to save innocent lives as much as we need shoot-to-kill. The judges' prohibition of all forms of torture has produced a ban on even discussing the use of any interrogation technique which might be effective. Although that helps the judges and us believe in our own moral integrity, it is not a safe way to protect ourselves from the terrorists who want to kill us.

When it comes to torture it is too easy to separate people into goodies and baddies—organisations like Amnesty International tend to dismiss as unrealistic any scenario where torture is the way to save hundreds of lives, but that is not responsible. The moral questions those scenarios illustrate need to be discussed. It's no good to lump people like Dershowitz and Yoo in with the people responsible for the torture at Abu Ghraib. Public wrath can easily extinguish all debate about torture while black sites, renditions and other crimes go on under the radar.

Enhanced Interrogation Is Justified If It Saves Lives

Peter Wehner

Peter Wehner is a senior fellow at the Ethics and Public Policy Center. He writes on political, cultural, religious, and national-security issues. He has been published in the New York Times, Wall Street Journal, Washington Post, *the* Atlantic, Financial Times, *the* Weekly Standard, Commentary, National Affairs, Christianity Today *and* Time *magazine.*

The issue of the Bush Administration's enhanced interrogation techniques involve several inter-related questions.

There is, first of all, the matter of morality. Critics of enhanced interrogation techniques have taken to saying that Americans don't torture, period—meaning in this instance that we do not engage in coercive interrogation techniques ranging from sleep deprivation to prolonged loud noise and/or bright lights to waterboarding. Anyone who holds the opposite view is a moral cretin and guilty of "arrant inhumanity." Or so the argument goes.

But this posture begins to come apart under examination. For one thing, the issue of "torture" itself needs to be put in a moral context and on a moral continuum. Waterboarding is a very nasty technique for sure—but it is considerably different (particularly in the manner administered by the CIA) than, say, mutilation with electric drills, rape, splitting knees, or forcing a terrorist to watch his children suffer and die in order to try to elicit information from him. Waterboarding is a technique that has been routinely used in the training of some U.S. military personnel—and which the journalist Christopher Hitchens endured. I certainly wouldn't want to undergo waterboarding—but while a very harsh technique,

"Morality and Enhanced Interrogation Techniques", by Peter Wehner, Commentary Magazine, April 27, 2009. Reprinted from COMMENTARY, April 2009 by permission; © 2017 by Commentary, Inc.

it is one that was applied in part because it would do far less damage to a person than other techniques. It is also surely relevant that waterboarding was not used randomly and promiscuously, but rather on three known terrorists. And of the thousands of unlawful combatants captured by the U.S., fewer than 100 were detained and questioned in the CIA program, according to Michael Hayden, President Bush's last CIA director, and former Attorney General Michael Mukasey—and of those, fewer than one-third were subjected to any of the techniques discussed in the memos on enhanced interrogation.

Morality also involves balancing ends and means. It is therefore relevant to take into account the possible benefits from the act of coercive interrogation techniques. Democratic Senator Charles Schumer, during a 2004 hearing on the subject of torture, put it this way. "There are times when we all get into high dudgeon" on this matter, Schumer said, but that we "ought to be reasonable about this." He then added this:

> I think there are probably very few people in this [Congressional hearing] room or in America who would say that torture should never, ever be used, particularly if thousands of lives are at stake. Take the hypothetical: if we knew that there was a nuclear bomb hidden in an American city and we believe that some kind of torture, fairly severe maybe, would give us a chance of finding that bomb before it went off, my guess is most Americans and most Senators, maybe all, would do what you have to do. So it's easy to sit back in the armchair and say that torture can never be used. But when you're in the fox hole, it's a very different deal. And I respect, I think we all respect the fact that the President's in the fox-hole every day. So he can hardly be blamed for asking you, or his White House counsel or the Department of Defense, to figure out when it comes to torture, what the law allows and when the law allows it, and what there is permission to do.

Senator Schumer noted, "We certainly don't want torture to be used willy-nilly... But we also don't want the situation like I mentioned in Chicago to preclude it."

Apropos of Schumer's comments, critics of enhanced interrogation techniques need to wrestle with a set of questions they like to avoid: if you knew using waterboarding against a known terrorist may well elicit information that would stop a massive attack on an American city, would you still insist it never be used? Do you oppose the use of waterboarding if it would save a thousand innocent lives? Ten thousand? A hundred thousand? What exactly is the point, if any, at which you believe waterboarding might be justified? I simply don't accept that those who answer "never" are taking a morally superior stand to those who answer "sometimes, in extremely rare circumstances and in very limited cases."

Let's consider the more common cases that don't involve a "ticking time bomb scenario." How might you react if you found yourself in government in the immediate aftermath of the attacks on 9/11, in which you knew al Qaeda was responsible for the strike and knew it was intent on doing far more damage to America. You captured a high-value terrorist who, if you elicit information from him, might well provide you with details that are essential to preventing a future attack and mass death. You are told enhanced interrogation techniques, if employed properly and under guidance, will work; and will probably save many thousands of innocent lives. In that case many people would, I think, (reluctantly) give the green light to coercive techniques—which is exactly what Congress, including Democratic Members of Congress, did.

On the substantive level, there is the question of the efficacy of enhanced interrogation techniques. There is an intense debate surrounding this matter, but we can certainly say that respected members of the intelligence world insist that innocent Americans are today alive because we employed a set of coercive interrogation techniques. According to Hayden and Mukasey, "As late as 2006, fully half of the government's knowledge about the structure and activities of Al Qaeda came from those interrogations." Former CIA Director George Tenet said, "I know that this program has saved lives. I know we've disrupted plots. I know this program alone is worth more than [what] the FBI, the [CIA], and the National

Security Agency put together have been able to tell us." And former National Intelligence Director Mike McConnell has said, "We have people walking around in this country that are alive today because this process happened."

Stuart Taylor, the politically moderate and intellectually honest columnist for National Journal, put it this way:

> The fashionable assumption that coercive interrogation (up to and including torture) never saved a single life makes it easy to resolve what otherwise would be an agonizing moral quandary. The same assumption makes it even easier for congressional Democrats, human-rights activists, and George W. Bush-hating avengers to call for prosecuting and imprisoning the former president and his entire national security team, including their lawyers. . . . But there is a body of evidence suggesting that brutal interrogation methods may indeed have saved lives, perhaps a great many lives—and that renouncing those methods may someday end up costing many, many more.

It seems unlikely that asking a jihadist his surname, first name and rank, date of birth, army, regimental, personal or serial number, or failing this, equivalent information—which is what the Geneva Conventions say ought to apply to prisoners of war but not, historically, to unlawful enemy combatants—would elicit as much information as coercive interrogation techniques. Dennis Blair, Obama's national intelligence director, admitted to his staff that "high value information came from interrogations in which those methods were used and provided a deeper understanding" of al Qaeda. (Once Blair's memo was revealed, he added this caveat: "There is no way of knowing whether the same information could have been obtained through other means.") And thanks to Taylor, we know that in 2002 the current Attorney General, Eric Holder, said that terrorists are not "entitled to the protection of the Geneva Convention" and that we need to "find out what their future plans might be, where other cells are located."

I am not one who believes that there is no cost to pursuing enhanced interrogation techniques. In debating policies, especially those that reach the president, there are costs and benefits to consider. So it's certainly possible that our employment of enhanced interrogation techniques was used as a recruitment tool for militant jihadists; if so, that needs to be weighed against the plots you break up and the innocent lives you save. Also, many members of the military oppose waterboarding because they feel it stains the reputation of America and endangers our own servicemen and women (though it's hard to accept the argument that al Qaeda would be less sadistic if we had not used coercive interrogation techniques; after all, they were beheading innocent people even before it was known the U.S. used water-boarding). These are not silly objections. Beyond that, most of us instinctively pull back from using harsh interrogation techniques and certainly torture. Given the double-obligation of morality and law, we should begin with the presumption that waterboarding shouldn't be utilized and then set a very high bar for anyone who would argue that it might be acceptable in very limited instances.

But that is, in fact, what seems to have occurred. And so I do not accept for a moment that the last eight years constitute a "dark chapter" in our history. Quite the opposite. Michael Gerson points out that our history is replete with actions—the firebombing of Dresden, dropping the atomic bomb on Hiroshima, and (I would add) Franklin Roosevelt's Executive Order 9066, which led to the internment of more than 100,000 Japanese Americans in World War II—which certainly raise more morally problematic issues than what the Bush Administration pursued.

There are of course serious-minded critics of enhanced interrogation techniques. But to pretend, as some critics do, that the morality of this issue is self-evident and that waterboarding and other coercive interrogation techniques are obviously unacceptable and something for which our nation should be ashamed is, in my judgment, not only wrong but irresponsible. When a nation is engaged in war, you hope to find in government sober people who are able to weigh competing moral goods and who take seriously their obligation to protect our nation. They may not get everything right at the time—hardly anyone does in the heat of the moment —but they should not have to face a lynch mob years after the fact (especially those in the lynch mob who blessed the activities at the time they were being used). The American public, one hopes, can see through all this. And as Nancy Pelosi might well discover, playing a role in inciting a mob can come at a cost.

Harsh Interrogation Techniques Are Necessary for the Greater Good

Michael Barone

Michael Barone is an American conservative political analyst, historian, and journalist. He is principal author of The Almanac of American Politics, *a reference work on Congress and state politics. He is also senior analyst for the* Washington Examiner.

When former Vice President Dan Quayle scheduled a big speech, President Bill Clinton didn't hop in and schedule one for the hour before. When former Vice President Al Gore scheduled a big speech, President George W. Bush didn't hop in and schedule one for the hour before. But when former Vice President Dick Cheney scheduled a big speech for 10:30 a.m. last week at the American Enterprise Institute, where I am a research fellow, President Barack Obama hopped in and scheduled a speech for 10 a.m. that day at the National Archives.

A little defensive, no?

Cheney spoke in defense of the Bush administration's terrorist interrogation policies and of the Guantanamo detention camp. But he was really on offense. The Bush administration managed to keep America safe for 2,689 days after the September 11 attacks, he said. The enhanced interrogation techniques, including waterboarding of three captured terrorists, saved hundreds of lives. Barack Obama's release of the legal memoranda approving those techniques has made our defenders less safe; now let him release the reports showing the information we got from the detainees.

"No Time for Tea-and-Crumpet Interrogations," by Michael Barone, American Enterprise Institute, May 24, 2009. Reprinted by permission.

Were the Enhanced Interrogations Really Terrible?

There were even a couple of well-deserved swipes at the press. The *New York Times*, Cheney noted, was "publishing secrets in a way that could only help al Qaeda. It impressed the Pulitzer committee, but it damn sure didn't serve the interests of our country, or the safety of our people." The *Times* reporter sitting behind me at AEI said afterwards he agreed; whether he was joking or serious I couldn't tell.

From Obama we heard a lawyerly defense of his acquiescence in Bush policies which he lambasted on the campaign trail, including his declaration that we will hold some detainees indefinitely without trial by civilian courts or military commissions. After urging that we not look backward, he did so himself, saying he inherited a "mess" and assuring us, without supporting data, that Guantanamo "likely created more terrorists around the world than it ever detained."

I have tried to understand the fury of the political Left, a fury Obama stoked in the Senate and on the campaign trail, over the interrogation techniques and Guantanamo. Yes, the interrogations were a miserable business, and I wouldn't like to be in the room for them, on either side of the questioning. But were they really terrible? You don't have to consult Mr. Webster to know that this is a distinction with a difference. September 11 was terrible. The terrorist attacks of the 1990s, which Cheney grimly ticked off, were terrible. I recently reread Gerhard Weinberg's brilliant history of World War II, *A World At Arms*, and in my comfortable chair could only begin to appreciate how terrible the conflict was for tens of millions.

The war against terrorism, like civilian law enforcement, is filled with no-win choices. I was in law school in the 1960s, when the Supreme Court was issuing decisions softening the treatment of criminal suspects. Those decisions were informed by the law review articles of University of Michigan law professor Yale Kamisar, which set forth the grim scenes of police grinding confessions out of (almost always guilty) defendants. From the Gothic compound of Michigan Law School or the quiet of a judge's chambers, those scenes seemed horrifying, something that just couldn't be allowed to happen.

And from leafy Ann Arbor of the serene Supreme Court building, the results of those decisions, and of the softened law enforcement of those years, may not have looked so bad. But I saw those results on the streets of Detroit, and they were ugly. Crime tripled in ten years. Thousands of people were murdered, beaten, robbed. Inner city neighborhoods were destroyed. You can go there today and see the burnt-out houses and empty lots and shells of commercial strips in what was once America's fourth largest city and which now has less than half the population it did in the 1950s.

I believe Barack Obama is taking seriously his responsibility to protect the nation. His speech at the Archives had some uplifting rhetoric, but it tottered between denunciations of the Bush administration and attempts to propitiate those in his own party who are angry that he is continuing military commissions and indefinite detention without trial–and those Democrats who voted last week to prohibit any Guantanamo detainees from being sent to the United States. I hope his continued denunciation of "torture" won't limit our defenders to tea-and-crumpets interrogations. And that he realizes now that we need something like Guantanamo.

Torture Can Never Be Morally Justified

Phil Lawler

Phil Lawler is a Catholic journalist. He has edited several Catholic magazines and written ten books. The founder of Catholic World News, *he is the news director and lead analyst at CatholicCulture.org.*

Some moral questions are very complicated. Others are very straightforward. In some cases, the morality of an act depends entirely on the circumstances. But some acts can never be justified, regardless of the circumstances.

The Catholic Church teaches quite clearly that some acts are intrinsically wrong. Deliberate abortion, for example, is always wrong. And so is torture.

This week's revelations about the "enhanced interrogation" techniques used by representatives of the US government in the war on terror should trouble the conscience of every American. Some of the measures used in questioning captives were brutal and degrading. How could they possibly be justified?

(We could also argue about whether lawmakers who were fully briefed on these interrogation tactics a decade ago are in a strong position to criticize them now. And we could argue whether it is irresponsible to issue a public report on these unsavory tactics—likely inflaming passions against the US and endangering Americans serving abroad—rather than quietly punishing the culprits. But those are debates for another day.)

In light of this week's revelations, the burden of proof is on those who contend that agents of the US government did *not* use torture. The world at large believes that they did. We Americans cannot dismiss that belief lightly.

"Regardless of Circumstances or Results, Torture Can Never Be Morally Justified," by Phil Lawler, Trinity Communications, December 10, 2014. Reprinted by permission catholicculture.org.

We can, if we choose, blame the media for sensationalizing the report, and blame the politicians for exploiting the story. But if in fact our government's policies were gravely immoral, then we bear some degree of responsibility. To preserve our integrity (not to mention our souls), we must face that question directly.

Were American government agents authorized to use torture? It would take a strong stomach and a weak conscience to read descriptions of the CIA's questioning sessions without serious qualms. Keep in mind that in his encyclical *Veritatis Splendor*, St. John Paul II wrote that "physical *and mental* torture" is intrinsically evil. *(emphasis added).*

The *Catechism of the Catholic Church* (#2298) teaches: "Torture which uses physical or moral violence to extract confessions, punish the guilty, frighten opponents, or satisfy hatred is contrary to respect for the person and for human dignity." When an interrogator treats his captor in a degrading manner, the human dignity of both men is violated; by treating his subject as something less than human, the captor becomes something less than human himself.

Defenders of the "enhanced interrogation" techniques say that it was necessary to put extra pressure on terrorist suspects, to extract important information that would save the lives of innocent people. That is a powerful, practical argument. But is it true? Expert interrogators question that premise.

A tortured prisoner might blurt out… anything. He may tell the truth, or he may say whatever he thinks his questioner wants to hear, whether it is true or not. Under extreme duress, he might not even know whether he is telling the truth or not; when pushed beyond their endurance, most people become *less* capable of speaking intelligently.

Even if it were true that torture could induce prisoners to give more accurate information, that would not be enough to justify an intrinsically evil act. Some defense experts claim that "enhanced interrogation" helped to ward off terrorist attacks. That is, to be sure, a powerful practical argument. But practical arguments are not enough to justify an intrinsically immoral act. How many women, finding themselves in difficult pregnancies, can make powerful practical arguments in favor of abortion?

A moral end does not justify an immoral means. In our battle against terrorism we may think of ourselves as the representatives of all that is good, that we are on God's side. Yet we cannot claim the mantle of righteousness while using immoral means. The *Catechism* (#214*) warns: "It is also blasphemous to make use of God's name to cover up criminal practices, to reduce peoples to servitude, *to torture persons* or put them to death." *(emphasis added)*

Once we adopt immoral tactics, we lose our right to claim moral superiority over our adversaries. Our complaints about the brutality of terrorists will ring hollow if we engage in brutality ourselves. We cannot defeat terrorism by adopting its methods.

The Lesser of Two Evils Is Still Evil

Phil Lawler

Phil Lawler is a Catholic journalist. He has edited several Catholic magazines and written ten books. The founder of Catholic World News, he is the news director and lead analyst at CatholicCulture.org.

Many readers have responded, with questions and criticisms, to my argument last week that "Regardless of circumstances or results, torture can never be justified." Let me respond to some of the common concerns.

The Senate report on "enhanced interrogation" was a partisan document, released by liberals seeking to gain political advantage.

No doubt that's true, but it's not relevant to our discussion about the (im)morality of torture. The motives of the people publishing the report do not affect the accuracy of the facts contained therein. If some credible expert could assure me that the report is factually wrong or grossly exaggerated, I would be relieved. To date, unfortunately, I have not seen anyone seriously dispute the overall accuracy of the report.

How should torture be defined? Where should we draw the line between aggressive questioning of a hostile witness and outright torture?

In my original essay I skipped lightly over this important question, assuming that anyone who had read the Senate report would recognize that the line—wherever it is—had been crossed. If you can read the description of those "interrogation" techniques without qualms, I am grateful that I am not your prisoner.

"Can Torture Ever be Justified? Round II," by Phil Lawler, Trinity Communications, December 15, 2014. Reprinted by permission.

Still the question is worth asking: What is torture? Few rational people would argue that a suspected terrorist should be seated in a comfortable chair, given a cold drink, and addressed politely. Some degree of pressure can and should be exerted on the suspect, to prompt quick and accurate answers.

Torture, however, is the deliberate infliction of pain, intended not to secure the subject's cooperation but to break his will. The *Catechism of the Catholic Church* (#2298) conveys the sense of the term: "Torture which uses physical or moral violence to extract confessions, punish the guilty, frighten opponents, or satisfy hatred is contrary to respect for the person and for human dignity."

Perhaps one way to distinguish between legitimate tough questioning and torture would be to imagine how we would react if we learned that the subject of the interrogation was completely innocent: that he provided no information because he had no information to provide. If that innocent man had been made to sweat and squirm for a few hours, that would be unfortunate. But if he had been broken in body or in spirit, that, I suggest, would be torture.

The Catechism condemns torture when it is used to extract confessions. But in the war against terror, the CIA used "enhanced interrogation" to extract information that could be used in the fight against terrorism.

What distinction is being made here? In one case the suspect does not want to admit his guilt, but the torturer forces a confession out of him. In the other case the man does not want to provide information about his terrorist colleagues, but the torture pries that information out of him. The results are different but the motivation of the torturer is the same: to extract information that the subject will not willingly provide.

In *Veritatis Splendor* (80) St. John Paul II, citing Vatican II, lists "physical and mental torture and attempts to coerce the spirit" among the actions that "are by their nature 'incapable of being ordered' to God, because they radically contradict the good of the person made in his image."

But aren't some American soldiers subjected to the same sort of techniques (waterboarding, for instance) as part of their training, to prepare them to face hostile interrogation?

Yes, but these training sessions take place under controlled circumstances. Let's hope that the armed forces do not employ instructors who actually want to break the spirit of their trainees!

Motivation and intention are key factors in appraising the morality of an action—as well as the effect of that action on a human subject. Some medical procedures are painful and/or humiliating for the patient. We tolerate them because we realize that they are ultimately for our benefit, and because eventually we know the pain will stop. The subject of "enhanced interrogation" has no such assurances.

Maybe some interrogators used torture, but only because they "went rogue." Official US policy did not authorize such excesses.

This is actually a very important point, on which lawmakers should focus in light of the Senate report. Were a few interrogators going too far, or did their orders encourage them to do exactly what they did? There will always be some aggressive individuals who are tempted to slide over the line; that's why it's so important to draw a clear line at a morally defensible point. Did American leaders draw such a line? The televised remarks of former Vice President Cheney are not reassuring on this point.

But as Cheney said, the rough interrogation techniques were necessary; they saved American lives.

What is freely asserted can be freely denied. Some people say that the CIA interrogators extracted some information that could not have been obtained otherwise, thereby stopping terrorist attacks. Others say that the results of the "enhanced interrogation" were meager. It is impossible to know what might have happened under other circumstances.

In general, are Americans—is the world—safer now than a decade ago? Has the threat of terrorism waxed or waned? Maybe the use of torture produced information that enabled our forces to stop *x* number of terrorist attacks. But could the resentment and rage provoked by the torture turned young men toward terrorism, so that now we face *2x* or *3x* more attacks? Those calculations, too, cannot be resolved with the information that we have on hand.

And in any case, the calculus of success and failure, even measured in human lives, does not answer the key question here. If torture is intrinsically wrong—if it can never be justified, regardless of the circumstances—then it must be rejected.

Doesn't just-war theory allow us to choose the lesser of two evils?

No. The lesser of two evils is still evil. Again, if something is intrinsically wrong, it is wrong in all circumstances.

The tradition of just-war teaching allows for the use of proportionate force to stop an unjust aggressor. Under some circumstances, when other remedies have proven ineffective, the Catholic teaching on justice in warfare allows for the use of lethal force. But even when lethal force is employed, it is never justifiable to hate an enemy or deliberately to strip him of his dignity.

Even in all-out war, the Church teaches that some options— such as the deliberately targeting of civilians—are morally unjustifiable. That clear, universal, moral imperative lies at the heart of our condemnation of terrorism. Even if they had a just cause, we would still condemn them for shedding innocent blood.

St. John Paul II used his personalist philosophy to explain the principle at work here. A human person can never be treated as an object: a means toward an end. It is always wrong to say, "I will kill these innocent people in order to change the policies of that government." It is also wrong to say, "I will inflict hideous pain on this person in order to extract information that will thwart the plans of these other people."

Al Qaida, the Taliban, the Islamic State, and other terrorist organizations routinely target innocent civilians. Their methods are far more immoral than the excesses of the CIA. There is no moral equivalence here.

True. The CIA's offenses are not nearly as egregious as those of Al Qaida, the Taliban, and the Islamic State. Is that supposed to be reassuring? If we justify our policies by comparing them with those of avowed killers, we have come a long way from the "shining city on a hill."

The Enhanced Interrogation Program Revealed a Monstrous Morality

Paul Waldman

Paul Waldman is a weekly columnist and senior writer for the American Prospect. *He also writes for the* Washington Post *and the* Week *and is the author of* Being Right is Not Enough: What Progressives Must Learn From Conservative Success.

This morning, *The Washington Post* has a blockbuster story about that 6,300-page Senate Intelligence Committee report on the CIA's torture program. The part that will likely get the most attention is the conclusion that torture produced little if any useful intelligence, which is extremely important. But even more damning is the picture the committee paints of a CIA that all along was trying to convince everyone that what they were doing was effective, even as it failed to produce results. I have a post on this over at the *Post* this morning, but I want to elaborate on this aspect of the story. This is a tale of moral sunk costs, and how people react when they've sold their souls and realize that they won't even get paid what they bargained for.

In case you're unfamiliar with the economic idea of sunk costs it's basically the idea of throwing good money after bad: once you've gone down a particular path, what you've already invested (money, time, effort) acts as an emotional tug preventing you from abandoning that path even if a more rational assessment would dictate that you change course.

In the case of the CIA (and the Bush administration), they had a moral sunk cost in the torture program. They had made an extraordinary ethical choice, to make torture the official policy of the United States (and renaming it "enhanced interrogation" wasn't

"The CIA and the Moral Sunk Costs of the Torture Program," by Paul Waldman, The American Prospect, April 1, 2014. Reprinted by permission.

going to fool anyone, not even themselves). Once that decision was made and the torture began, it *had* to be effective, and not just effective but *fantastically* effective, in order to justify the moral compromise they had made. When the torture program failed to produce the results they hoped for, they could have said, "This stuff isn't working; let's focus on what does." But by then they couldn't retreat; the only hope of balancing the moral scales was to go forward. They were probably hoping that if they just kept on torturing, eventually it would produce something helpful and the whole program could be justified. But in the meantime, they'd try to fool people into thinking it was working splendidly:

> One official said that almost all of the critical threat-related information from Abu Zubaida was obtained during the period when he was questioned by [FBI interrogator Ali] Soufan at a hospital in Pakistan, well before he was interrogated by the CIA and waterboarded 83 times.
>
> Information obtained by Soufan, however, was passed up through the ranks of the U.S. intelligence community, the Justice Department and Congress as though it were part of what CIA interrogators had obtained, according to the committee report.
>
> "The CIA conflated what was gotten when, which led them to misrepresent the effectiveness of the program," said a second U.S. official who has reviewed the report. The official described the persistence of such misstatements as among "the most damaging" of the committee's conclusions...
>
> The committee described a similar sequence in the interrogation of Hassan Ghul, an al-Qaeda operative who provided a critical lead in the search for bin Laden: the fact that the al-Qaeda leader's most trusted courier used the moniker "al-Kuwaiti."
>
> But Ghul disclosed that detail while being interrogated by Kurdish authorities in northern Iraq who posed questions scripted by CIA analysts. The information from that period was subsequently conflated with lesser intelligence gathered from Ghul at a secret CIA prison in Romania, officials said. Ghul was later turned over to authorities in Pakistan, where

he was subsequently released. He was killed by a CIA drone strike in 2012.

So over and over, the CIA is attributing information they got through ordinary interrogation to torture. If the torture program was even marginally effective, there would be no need to do so; it wouldn't be threatened by the fact that some information came from other means, so long as torture was producing some other information as well. Only if the torture program was useless would it become necessary to lie about it.

The picture this paints is one of an agency that is simultaneously torturing prisoners, without much effect, and also trying desperately to tell a story to the rest of the government that the torture is working. And to this day, everyone on up the chain— most recently Dick Cheney, who said the other day of the torture program that he'd do it all over again, because "The results speak for themselves"—insists the same thing. Because if it didn't work, what are they? They're monsters. They transgressed one of humanity's most profound moral injunctions, for nothing. And no one wants to believe that about themselves.

CHAPTER 3

Is Enhanced Interrogation Just Another Name for Torture?

Overview: The US Enhanced Interrogation Program Is Problematic

Alfred W. McCoy

Alfred W. McCoy is the JRW Smail professor of history at the University of Wisconsin–Madison. His many books include Policing America's Empire *and* A Question of Torture.

I f, like me, you've been following America's torture policies not just for the last few years, but for decades, you can't help but experience that eerie feeling of déjà vu these days. With the departure of George W. Bush and Dick Cheney from Washington and the arrival of Barack Obama, it may just be back to the future when it comes to torture policy, a turn away from a dark, do-it-yourself ethos and a return to the outsourcing of torture that went on, with the support of both Democrats and Republicans, in the Cold War years.

Like Chile after the regime of General Augusto Pinochet or the Philippines after the dictatorship of Ferdinand Marcos, Washington after Bush is now trapped in the painful politics of impunity. Unlike anything our allies have experienced, however, for Washington, and so for the rest of us, this may prove a political crisis without end or exit.

Despite dozens of official inquiries in the five years since the Abu Ghraib photos first exposed our abuse of Iraqi detainees, the torture scandal continues to spread like a virus, infecting all who touch it, including now Obama himself. By embracing a specific methodology of torture, covertly developed by the CIA over decades using countless millions of taxpayer dollars and graphically revealed in those Iraqi prison photos, we have condemned ourselves to retreat from whatever promises might be

"Back to the Future in Torture Policy," by Alfred W. McCoy, Tom Dispatch.com, June 8, 2009. http://www.tomdispatch.com/post/175080. Reprinted by permission.

made to end this sort of abuse and are instead already returning to a bipartisan consensus that made torture America's secret weapon throughout the Cold War.

Despite the 24 version of events, the Bush administration did not simply authorize traditional, bare-knuckle torture. What it did do was develop to new heights the world's most advanced form of psychological torture, while quickly recognizing the legal dangers in doing so. Even in the desperate days right after 9/11, the White House and Justice Department lawyers who presided over the Bush administration's new torture program were remarkably punctilious about cloaking their decisions in legalisms designed to preempt later prosecution.

To most Americans, whether they supported the Bush administration torture policy or opposed it, all of this seemed shocking and very new. Not so, unfortunately. Concealed from Congress and the public, the CIA had spent the previous half-century developing and propagating a sophisticated form of psychological torture meant to defy investigation, prosecution, or prohibition—and so far it has proved remarkably successful on all these counts. Even now, since many of the leading psychologists who worked to advance the CIA's torture skills have remained silent, we understand surprisingly little about the psychopathology of the program of mental torture that the Bush administration applied so globally.

Physical torture is a relatively straightforward matter of sadism that leaves behind broken bodies, useless information, and clear evidence for prosecution. Psychological torture, on the other hand, is a mind maze that can destroy its victims, even while entrapping its perpetrators in an illusory, almost erotic, sense of empowerment. When applied skillfully, it leaves few scars for investigators who might restrain this seductive impulse. However, despite all the myths of these last years, psychological torture, like its physical counterpart, has proven an ineffective, even counterproductive, method for extracting useful information from prisoners.

Where it has had a powerful effect is on those ordering and delivering it. With their egos inflated beyond imagining by a sense of being masters of life and death, pain and pleasure, its perpetrators, when in office, became forceful proponents of abuse, striding across the political landscape like Nietzschean supermen. After their fall from power, they have continued to maneuver with extraordinary determination to escape the legal consequences of their actions.

Before we head deeper into the hidden history of the CIA's psychological torture program, however, we need to rid ourselves of the idea that this sort of torture is somehow "torture lite" or merely, as the Bush administration renamed it, "enhanced interrogation." Although seemingly less brutal than physical methods, psychological torture actually inflicts a crippling trauma on its victims. "Ill treatment during captivity, such as psychological manipulations and forced stress positions," Dr. Metin Basoglu has reported in the Archives of General Psychiatry after interviewing 279 Bosnian victims of such methods, "does not seem to be substantially different from physical torture in terms of the severity of mental suffering."

A Secret History of Psychological Torture

The roots of our present paralysis over what to do about detainee abuse lie in the hidden history of the CIA's program of psychological torture. Early in the Cold War, panicked that the Soviets had somehow cracked the code of human consciousness, the Agency mounted a "Special Interrogation Program" whose working hypothesis was: "Medical science, particularly psychiatry and psychotherapy, has developed various techniques by means of which some external control can be imposed on the mind/ or will of an individual, such as drugs, hypnosis, electric shock and neurosurgery."

All of these methods were tested by the CIA in the 1950s and 1960s. None proved successful for breaking potential enemies or obtaining reliable information. Beyond these ultimately unsuccessful methods, however, the Agency also explored a behavioral approach to cracking that "code." In 1951, in collaboration with British and Canadian defense scientists, the Agency encouraged academic research into "methods concerned in psychological coercion." Within months, the Agency had defined the aims of its top-secret program, code-named Project Artichoke, as the "development of any method by which we can get information from a person against his will and without his knowledge."

This secret research produced two discoveries central to the CIA's more recent psychological paradigm. In classified experiments, famed Canadian psychologist Donald Hebb found that he could induce a state akin to drug-induced hallucinations and psychosis in just 48 hours—without drugs, hypnosis, or electric shock. Instead, for two days student volunteers at McGill University simply sat in a comfortable cubicle deprived of sensory stimulation by goggles, gloves, and earmuffs. "It scared the hell out of us," Hebb said later, "to see how completely dependent the mind is on a close connection with the ordinary sensory environment, and how disorganizing to be cut off from that support."

During the 1950s, two neurologists at Cornell Medical Center, under CIA contract, found that the most devastating torture technique of the Soviet secret police, the KGB, was simply to force a victim to stand for days while the legs swelled, the skin erupted in suppurating lesions, and hallucinations began—a procedure which we now politely refer to as "stress positions."

Four years into this project, there was a sudden upsurge of interest in using mind control techniques defensively after American prisoners in North Korea suffered what was then called "brainwashing." In August 1955, President Eisenhower ordered that any soldier at risk of capture should be given "specific training and instruction designed to... withstand all enemy efforts against him."

Consequently, the Air Force developed a program it dubbed SERE (Survival, Evasion, Resistance, Escape) to train pilots in resisting psychological torture. In other words, two intertwined strands of research into torture methods were being explored and developed: aggressive methods for breaking enemy agents and defensive methods for training Americans to resist enemy inquisitors.

In 1963, the CIA distilled its decade of research into the curiously named KUBARK Counter-intelligence Interrogation manual, which stated definitively that sensory deprivation was effective because it made "the regressed subject view the interrogator as a father-figure... strengthening... the subject's tendencies toward compliance." Refined through years of practice on actual human beings, the CIA's psychological paradigm now relies on a mix of sensory overload and deprivation via seemingly banal procedures: the extreme application of heat and cold, light and dark, noise and silence, feast and famine—all meant to attack six essential sensory pathways into the human mind.

After codifying its new interrogation methods in the KUBARK manual, the Agency spent the next 30 years promoting these torture techniques within the U.S. intelligence community and among anti-communist allies. In its clandestine journey across continents and decades, the CIA's psychological torture paradigm would prove elusive, adaptable, devastatingly destructive, and powerfully seductive. So darkly seductive is torture's appeal that these seemingly scientific methods, even when intended for a few Soviet spies or al-Qaeda terrorists, soon spread uncontrollably in two directions—toward the torture of the many and into a paroxysm of brutality towards specific individuals. During the Vietnam War, when the CIA applied these techniques in their search for information on top Vietcong cadre, the interrogation effort soon degenerated into the crude physical brutality of the Phoenix Program, producing 46,000 extrajudicial executions and little actionable intelligence.

In 1994, with the Cold War over, Washington ratified the U.N. Convention Against Torture, seemingly resolving the tension between its anti-torture principles and its torture practices. Yet when President Clinton sent this Convention to Congress, he included four little-noticed diplomatic "reservations" drafted six years before by the Reagan administration and focused on just one word in those 26 printed pages: "mental."

These reservations narrowed (just for the United States) the definition of "mental" torture to include just four acts: the infliction of physical pain, the use of drugs, death threats, or threats to harm another. Excluded were methods such as sensory deprivation and self-inflicted pain, the very techniques the CIA had propagated for the past 40 years. This definition was reproduced verbatim in Section 2340 of the U.S. Federal Code and later in the War Crimes Act of 1996. Through this legal legerdemain, Washington managed to agree, via the U.N. Convention, to ban physical abuse even while exempting the CIA from the U.N.'s prohibition on psychological torture.

This little noticed exemption was left buried in those documents like a landmine and would detonate with phenomenal force just 10 years later at Abu Ghraib prison.

War on Terror, War of Torture

Right after his public address to a shaken nation on September 11, 2001, President Bush gave his staff secret orders to pursue torture policies, adding emphatically, "I don't care what the international lawyers say, we are going to kick some ass." In a dramatic break with past policy, the White House would even allow the CIA to operate its own global network of prisons, as well as charter air fleet to transport seized suspects and "render" them for endless detention in a supranational gulag of secret "black sites" from Thailand to Poland.

The Bush administration also officially allowed the CIA ten "enhanced" interrogation methods designed by agency psychologists, including "waterboarding." This use of cold water to block breathing triggers the "mammalian diving reflex," hardwired into every human brain, thus inducing an uncontrollable terror of impending death.

As Jane Mayer reported in the New Yorker, psychologists working for both the Pentagon and the CIA "reverse engineered" the military's SERE training, which included a brief exposure to waterboarding, and flipped these defensive methods for use offensively on al-Qaeda captives. "They sought to render the detainees vulnerable—to break down all of their senses," one official told Mayer. "It takes a psychologist trained in this to understand these rupturing experiences." Inside Agency headquarters, there was, moreover, a "high level of anxiety" about the possibility of future prosecutions for methods officials knew to be internationally defined as torture. The presence of Ph.D. psychologists was considered one "way for CIA officials to skirt measures such as the Convention Against Torture."

From recently released Justice Department memos, we now know that the CIA refined its psychological paradigm significantly under Bush. As described in the classified 2004 Background Paper on the CIA's Combined Use of Interrogation Techniques, each detainee was transported to an Agency black site while "deprived of sight and sound through the use of blindfolds, earmuffs, and hoods." Once inside the prison, he was reduced to "a baseline, dependent state" through conditioning by "nudity, sleep deprivation (with shackling...), and dietary manipulation."

For "more physical and psychological stress," CIA interrogators used coercive measures such as "an insult slap or abdominal slap" and then "walling," slamming the detainee's head against a cell wall. If these failed to produce the results sought, interrogators escalated to waterboarding, as was done to Abu Zubaydah "at least 83 times during August 2002" and Khalid Sheikh Mohammad 183 times in March 2003—so many times, in fact, that the repetitiousness of the act can only be considered convincing testimony to the seductive sadism of CIA-style torture.

In a parallel effort launched by Bush-appointed civilians in the Pentagon, Secretary of Defense Donald Rumsfeld gave General Geoffrey Miller command of the new American military prison at Guantanamo in late 2002 with ample authority to transform it into an ad hoc psychology lab. Behavioral Science Consultation Teams of military psychologists probed detainees for individual phobias like fear of the dark. Interrogators stiffened the psychological assault by exploiting what they saw as Arab cultural sensitivities when it came to sex and dogs. Via a three-phase attack on the senses, on culture, and on the individual psyche, interrogators at Guantanamo perfected the CIA's psychological paradigm.

After General Miller visited Iraq in September 2003, the U.S. commander there, General Ricardo Sanchez, ordered Guantanamo-style abuse at Abu Ghraib prison. My own review of the 1,600 still-classified photos taken by American guards at Abu Ghraib—which journalists covering this story seem to share like Napster downloads—reveals not random, idiosyncratic acts by "bad apples," but the repeated, constant use of just three psychological techniques: hooding for sensory deprivation, shackling for self-inflicted pain, and (to exploit Arab cultural sensitivities) both nudity and dogs. It is no accident that Private Lynndie England was famously photographed leading an Iraqi detainee leashed like a dog.

These techniques, according to the New York Times, then escalated virally at five Special Operations field interrogation centers where detainees were subjected to extreme sensory deprivation, beating, burning, electric shock, and waterboarding. Among the thousand soldiers in these units, 34 were later convicted of abuse and many more escaped prosecution only because records were officially "lost."

"Behind the Green Door" at the White House

Further up the chain of command, National Security Advisor Condoleezza Rice, as she recently told the Senate, "convened a series of meetings of NSC [National Security Council] principals in 2002 and 2003 to discuss various issues... relating to detainees." This group, including Vice President Cheney, Attorney General John Ashcroft, Secretary of State Colin Powell, and CIA director George Tenet, met dozens of times inside the White House Situation Room.

After watching CIA operatives mime what Rice called "certain physical and psychological interrogation techniques," these leaders, their imaginations stimulated by graphic visions of human suffering, repeatedly authorized extreme psychological techniques stiffened by hitting, walling, and waterboarding. According to an April 2008 ABC News report, Attorney General Ashcroft once interrupted this collective fantasy by asking aloud, "Why are we talking about this in the White House? History will not judge this kindly."

In mid-2004, even after the Abu Ghraib photos were released, these principals met to approve the use of CIA torture techniques on still more detainees. Despite mounting concerns about the damage torture was doing to America's standing, shared by Colin Powell, Condoleezza Rice commanded Agency officials with the cool demeanor of a dominatrix. "This is your baby," she reportedly said. "Go do it."

Cleansing Torture

Even as they exercise extraordinary power over others, perpetrators of torture around the world are assiduous in trying to cover their tracks. They construct recondite legal justifications, destroy records of actual torture, and paper the files with spurious claims of success. Hence, the CIA destroyed 92 interrogation videotapes, while Vice President Cheney now berates Obama incessantly (five times in his latest Fox News interview) to declassify "two reports" which he claims will show the informational gains that torture offered —possibly because his staff salted the files at the NSC or the CIA with documents prepared for this very purpose.

Not only were Justice Department lawyers aggressive in their advocacy of torture in the Bush years, they were meticulous from the start, in laying the legal groundwork for later impunity. In three torture memos from May 2005 that the Obama administration recently released, Bush's Deputy Assistant Attorney General Stephen Bradbury repeatedly cited those original U.S. diplomatic "reservations" to the U.N. Convention Against Torture, replicated in Section 2340 of the Federal code, to argue that waterboarding was perfectly legal since the "technique is not physically painful." Anyway, he added, careful lawyering at Justice and the CIA had punched loopholes in both the U.N. Convention and U.S. law so wide that these Agency techniques were "unlikely to be subject to judicial inquiry."

Just to be safe, when Vice President Cheney presided over the drafting of the Military Commissions Act of 2006, he included clauses, buried in 38 pages of dense print, defining "serious physical pain" as the "significant loss or impairment of the function of a bodily member, organ, or mental faculty." This was a striking paraphrase of the outrageous definition of physical torture as pain "equivalent in intensity to... organ failure, impairment of bodily function, or even death" in John Yoo's infamous August 2002 "torture memo," already repudiated by the Justice Department.

Above all, the Military Commissions Act protected the CIA's use of psychological torture by repeating verbatim the exculpatory language found in those Clinton-era, Reagan-created reservations to the U.N. Convention and still embedded in Section 2340 of the Federal code. To make doubly sure, the act also made these definitions retroactive to November 1997, giving CIA interrogators immunity from any misdeeds under the Expanded War Crimes Act of 1997 which punishes serious violations with life imprisonment or death.

No matter how twisted the process, impunity—whether in England, Indonesia, or America—usually passes through three stages:

1. Blame the supposed "bad apples."
2. Invoke the security argument. ("It protected us.")
3. Appeal to national unity. ("We need to move forward together.")

For a year after the Abu Ghraib exposé, Rumsfeld's Pentagon blamed various low-ranking bad apples by claiming the abuse was "perpetrated by a small number of U.S. military." In his statement on May 13th, while refusing to release more torture photos, President Obama echoed Rumsfeld, claiming the abuse in these latest images, too, "was carried out in the past by a small number of individuals."

In recent weeks, Republicans have taken us deep into the second stage with Cheney's statements that the CIA's methods "prevented the violent deaths of thousands, perhaps hundreds of thousands, of people."

Then, on April 16th, President Obama brought us to the final stage when he released the four Bush-era memos detailing CIA torture, insisting: "Nothing will be gained by spending our time and energy laying blame for the past." During a visit to CIA headquarters four days later, Obama promised that there would be no prosecutions of Agency employees. "We've made some mistakes," he admitted, but urged Americans simply to "acknowledge them and then move forward." The president's statements were in such blatant defiance of international law that the U.N.'s chief official on torture, Manfred Nowak, reminded him that Washington was actually obliged to investigate possible violations of the Convention Against Torture.

This process of impunity is leading Washington back to a global torture policy that, during the Cold War, was bipartisan in nature: publicly advocating human rights while covertly outsourcing torture to allied governments and their intelligence agencies. In retrospect, it may become ever more apparent that the real aberration of the Bush years lay not in torture policies per se, but in the President's order that the CIA should operate its own torture prisons. The advantage of the bipartisan torture consensus of the Cold War era was, of course, that it did a remarkably good job most of the time of insulating Washington from the taint of torture, which was sometimes remarkably widely practiced.

There are already some clear signs of a policy shift in this direction in the Obama era. Since mid-2008, U.S. intelligence has captured a half-dozen al-Qaeda suspects and, instead of shipping them to Guantanamo or to CIA secret prisons, has had them interrogated by allied Middle Eastern intelligence agencies. Showing that this policy is again bipartisan, Obama's new CIA director Leon Panetta announced that the Agency would continue to engage in the rendition of terror suspects to allies like Libya, Pakistan, or Saudi Arabia where we can, as he put it, "rely on diplomatic assurances of good treatment." Showing the quality of such treatment, Time magazine reported on May 24th that Ibn al-Sheikh al-Libi, who famously confessed under torture that Saddam Hussein had provided al-Qaeda with chemical weapons and later admitted his lie to Senate investigators, had committed "suicide" in a Libyan cell.

The Price of Impunity

This time around, however, a long-distance torture policy may not provide the same insulation as in the past for Washington. Any retreat into torture by remote-control is, in fact, only likely to produce the next scandal that will do yet more damage to America's international standing.

Over a 40-year period, Americans have found themselves mired in this same moral quagmire on six separate occasions: following exposés of CIA-sponsored torture in South Vietnam (1970), Brazil (1974), Iran (1978), Honduras (1988), and then throughout Latin America (1997). After each exposé, the public's shock soon faded, allowing the Agency to resume its dirty work in the shadows.

Unless some formal inquiry is convened to look into a sordid history that reached its depths in the Bush era, and so begins to break this cycle of deceit, exposé, and paralysis followed by more of the same, we're likely, a few years hence, to find ourselves right back where we are now. We'll be confronted with the next American torture scandal from some future iconic dungeon, part of a dismal, ever lengthening procession that has led from the tiger cages of South Vietnam through the Shah of Iran's prison cells in Tehran to Abu Ghraib and the prison at Bagram Air Base in Afghanistan.

The next time, however, the world will not have forgotten those photos from Abu Ghraib. The next time, the damage to this country will be nothing short of devastating.

Waterboarding Is Torture

Naureen Shah

Naureen Shah is the senior director of campaigns at the US section of Amnesty International. Her analysis has recently been cited in coverage by the New York Times, Washington Post, LA Times, *and* Reuters, *among other outlets.*

For years, Amnesty International has witnessed public figures repeating misconceptions and inaccuracies about waterboarding. This American debate on torture has mostly got it wrong—here are three realities you need to know:

1. Waterboarding is slow-motion suffocation

People who take the time to learn about Waterboarding see how horrific it is.

But many people don't. Media and public figures often describe waterboarding as a form of "enhanced interrogation"—a euphemism that rationalizes and sanitizes torture.

As Malcolm Nance, combat veteran and former chief of training at the U.S. Navy Survival, Evasion, Resistance and Escape School, wrote here:

> Unless you have been strapped down to the board, have endured the agonizing feeling of the water overpowering your gag reflex, and then feel your throat open and allow pint after pint of water to involuntarily fill your lungs, you will not know the meaning of the word.

And as he told Congress:

"Waterboarding Is Torture: 3 Things You Need to Know," by Naureen Shah, Amnesty International USA, February 10, 2016. Reprinted by permission.

Waterboarding is slow-motion suffocation with enough time to contemplate the inevitability of blackout and expiration— usually the person goes into hysterics on the board…When done right it is controlled death.

Though the *New York Times* has abandoned the term "enhanced interrogation," much of the mainstream media are still using it.

2. The atrocities of the armed group calling itself Islamic State and other armed groups don't make waterboarding okay

Many think this: however abusive the United States may be, it doesn't rival its enemies. And implicitly if not explicitly: torture and other human rights abuses might be justified in light of the atrocities committed by armed groups like the one calling itself Islamic State.

This is a theme that popular culture indulges in, especially the post-9/11 genre of national security thriller shows like *24* and *Homeland*.

If "Homeland" reflects conventional wisdom, it's that yes, the U.S. is doing terrible things to people—in the face, though, of some really terrible things being done by other people.

Especially since the *Charlie Hebdo* attacks, we've witnessed a renewed sense of uncertainty and ambiguity about human rights in policy debates. In the U.S. and in countries around the world, we're hearing questions like:

- Mass surveillance is an invasion of privacy, but don't we need it to prevent terror attacks?
- Freedom of expression is important, but should people really be allowed to promote extremist views?
- And of course: torture and indefinite detention without charge are wrong, but shouldn't they be available tools, in limited circumstances, in case they're needed?

In some ways, these questions reflect a genuine need people have for security, especially in the face of attacks by armed groups and individuals.

Many public figures are posing security and human rights as a novel dilemma. But we should all take a breath. These aren't new questions, not really.

People the world over have faced the issue of how to respond to war, atrocities, and crises—for decades. The international human rights system was built after World War II as a repudiation of its horrors by developing human rights protections.

So, **no public figure should be claiming that the answer to human rights abuses is to commit still more human rights abuses.** That's an idea the world rejected a long time ago.

3. Whether torture "works" is the WRONG question

Many public figures have argued that torture "works." In the aftermath of the Senate report on torture published last December, that question has dominated media debates. Former CIA officials released a book about the Senate torture report criticizing its findings that torture was ineffective.

But what does it mean to say "torture works"? Works how, according to what metric?

Torture is not only illegal, it has had disastrous and far-reaching consequences: it has stained the U.S. government's reputation and undermined its credibility to promote respect for human rights. According to some in the military, it has put U.S. armed forces at risk.

Matthew Alexander, a former U.S. interrogator in Iraq, writes here that "**torture and abuse costs American lives**":

> I learned in Iraq that the No. 1 reason foreign fighters flocked there to fight were the abuses carried out at Abu Ghraib and Guantanamo. Our policy of torture was directly and swiftly recruiting fighters for al-Qaeda in Iraq…It's no exaggeration to say that at least half of our losses and casualties in that country have come at the hands of foreigners who joined the fray because of our program of detainee abuse.

The number of U.S. soldiers who have died because of our torture policy will never be definitively known, but it is fair to say that it is close to the number of lives lost on Sept. 11, 2001. How anyone can say that torture keeps Americans safe is beyond me—unless you don't count American soldiers as Americans.

Enhanced Interrogation Has Not Made America Safer

David Irvine

David Irvine is a former Republican state legislator and a retired Army brigadier general.

A few years ago, I served as a member of the Constitution Project's Task Force on Detainee Treatment—an 11-member, bi-partisan group of former, high-ranking officials in the judiciary, Congress, the diplomatic service, law enforcement, and the military —and other experts in medicine, law, and ethics. We conducted an exhaustive, nearly 3-year study of information available in the public record about the interrogation and treatment of detainees in Iraq, Afghanistan, Guantanamo, and the other CIA black sites. We conducted interviews with more than 100 individuals in the United States and overseas who had first-hand knowledge of American practices and policies, including military and intelligence officers, interrogators, policymakers, and former detainees. I interviewed three former Guantanamo prisoners in London: Moazzam Begg, Bishar al-Rawi, and Omar Deghayes.

Our study produced what was at the time the most comprehensive history and analysis of U.S. detention and interrogation practices from 2001 that was based on open source material. The conclusions of our report mirror the findings of the Senate Select Committee on Intelligence's (SSCI) summarized report on CIA torture, released today. Two points of agreement are especially significant.

First, the SSCI report and our report both confirm that the "enhanced interrogation techniques" (a euphemism for torture and coercive interrogation) reveal a brutality that shocks the conscience.

"Torture: Unreliable and Inestimably Costly," by David Irvine, Just Security, December 9, 2014. Reprinted by permission.

The SSCI report does not use the word torture, and I should note that when we began our work at The Constitution Project, we were undecided if we should use that term to describe what was done by our government on our behalf. By the end of our three-year project, our task force voted unanimously to use the word torture to describe the cruel, inhuman, and degrading treatment of detainees. Our consciences were shaken. Yours should be, too.

Americans, and those acting as our agents, have used: electricity; lighted cigarettes; freezing temperatures; withholding medical treatment; forced nudity; sexual humiliation; object rape; beatings with enough violence to break bones; prolonged sleep deprivation and interrogation; mock executions; various forms of sensory deprivation to include confinement in coffin boxes; prolonged standing and suspension from ceilings and door frames to increase stress; threats of harm to family members; and waterboarding, which is not "simulated drowning" at all, it's physiological drowning. Indeed, the United States has prosecuted waterboarding as a war crime. It was not uncommon for multiple techniques to be used simultaneously.

Second, there is no firm or persuasive evidence, now either in the public or the classified records, that the widespread use of brutal and coercive interrogation techniques produced significant information of value. There is substantial evidence that much of the information adduced from the techniques was not useful or reliable. The proponents of coercive interrogation techniques have claimed over and over that waterboarding saved thousands of lives and prevented more terrorist attacks. Our report, and now the report of Senate Select Committee, which reviewed hundreds of thousands of classified documents, found nothing that convincingly supports that assertion. What was found were contradictory timelines of arrests, conventional interrogation, application of coercive interrogation, alleged confessions, arrests of co-conspirators, and information provided by other investigative agencies and foreign intelligence sources.

One of the "disrupted plots" most frequently cited by defenders of the CIA's program was the Library Towers plan to fly planes into Los Angeles skyscrapers—the discovery of which was attributed to the waterboarding of Khalid Sheik Mohammed (KSM) 183 times. Neither our investigation nor the SSCI's could find a definitive link tying that plot's break-up to the waterboarding of KSM. The plan was actually disrupted when Malaysian police arrested the cell leader more than a year before KSM was captured. The would-be pilot backed out. Moreover, in spite of the waterboarding, KSM said nothing about a different plot he had financed: the suicide bombing of a Marriott Hotel in Jakarta in 2003 that killed 11 people and wounded 81.

What is so disturbing is that there seems to have been a sustained and deliberate effort by the CIA to claim success from brutal interrogations when actual timelines, information gained, or contradictory details did not reasonably support such success claims. No less troubling were CIA's claims that coercive brutality produced no lasting physical or psychological damage. These latter issues are currently tying the military commission proceedings at Guantanamo in knots.

The Office of Legal Counsel in the Justice Department, and perhaps even the White House, were relying on such claims by CIA personnel when they justified these programs. They did this without any independent effort to verify the efficacy of brutality or its permanent medical and psychological damage, and no one had any interest in hearing of the legal pitfalls from the military Judge Advocates General.

I have a knowledge and bias about interrogation techniques. I was commissioned as an Army strategic intelligence officer. For 18 years I taught prisoner of war interrogation and military law for the Sixth U.S. Army Intelligence School. I have spent decades studying which interrogation techniques work, and which do not. The institutional experience, research, and science consistently point to the efficacy of rapport-based techniques and the unreliability of coercion.

It is tempting and easy to employ a false calculus when thinking about torture. If one assumes that a suspect is a terrorist who knows of a plot to murder 500 people, it's easy to dismiss a brutal interrogation as "he deserved worse!" If retribution is the object of an interrogation, then brutality has some appeal. But if what is really desired is vital intelligence, why employ an interrogation strategy that is more likely than not to make a suspect catatonic? Put that another way: if torture is the fastest way to truth, why isn't it standard practice in everyday criminal law? Child kidnapping can terrorize a community. Why not waterboard the suspects to save a child's life?

The reason the justice system disallows torture is not judicial faintness of heart. It is because torture is unreliable. People confess to crimes they didn't commit under the pressure of coercive interrogation. One study of proven false confessions shows that the average length of police interrogations in those instances is 16 straight hours. Mohammed al Qahtani was interrogated for 20 hours a day, every day, for three months.

New York City recently agreed to pay a $41 million civil rights settlement in the case of the Central Park Five. In 1989, five black teenagers were convicted of assaulting and gang-raping a jogger who nearly died from her injuries. They served a 40-year collective sentence, based solely on their video-taped confessions, in the presence of their parents—after prolonged and manipulative interrogations—confessions they later recanted. There was no physical or DNA evidence linking them to the crime. Years later another man confessed to the crime for which the teenagers served time, and in his case, the DNA was a perfect match.

Why do we assume that the kinds of coercive interrogation which lead to false confessions in everyday criminal law somehow lead to truth in national security investigations? Even if one claims, "the Constitution is not a suicide pact, and when it comes to terrorists, the ends justify the means"—the question of efficacy doesn't go away. Instead, it becomes even more compelling. That's because using techniques that are more likely to produce useless information heightens risk. A rational system seeks to minimize the risks of false confessions.

Another piece of the torture calculus dismissed by its proponents is this: how many terrorist suspects, who may know nothing at all, is it permissible to rack in search of the persons you're really looking for? Two? Ten? Twenty? Fifty? And how does American exceptionalism right that injustice when the wrong person is tormented? So far, we've ignored these questions and counted on the courts to dismiss such legal claims based on official secrets defenses.

The SSCI report may well be the most comprehensive assessment of torture's efficacy that policymakers and the American public will ever have.

Here's why that matters. For more than ten years, Americans were told: (a) we didn't torture anyone; (b) the interrogations we conducted produced vital intelligence that saved tens of thousands of lives; and (c) it's a dirty but necessary job, similar to the argument made by Colonel Nathan Jessup in "A Few Good Men."

The Jessups out there are, by and large, a well-educated bunch. Many hold advanced degrees from prestigious institutions. They argue, "We followed orders and we were told it was lawful—and now, wusses are trying to hang us out." Is it asking too much to expect the elites in government and its secret services to recognize and follow the law and the Constitution rather than conspire to subvert it? Instead, we expect infantry privates and sergeants, who are very young, and few of whom have had advanced educational opportunities, to understand and refuse to follow an unlawful order in combat.

The SSCI report should be the start of a serious political discussion the nation has never been forced to have – that the Jessups fervently wish to avoid. A truly great nation will act like one. The CIA's interrogation program was rooted in the practices of Nazi Germany, the Soviet Union, Communist China, and North Korea. The template did not make America safer, and we will be paying for those mistakes for decades to come. Moazzam Begg put it succinctly: "Guantanamo and torture has cost America an entire generation of Muslim youth, all over the world. Close it, don't close it, it doesn't matter; you're too late." Only in this case it's not too late. With the release of the key findings in the SSCI report, we finally have a chance to show the American people and the world that torture wasn't worth it, and that we ought never go down that path again. Better yet, Congress and the President should come together and pass legislation to reaffirm the prohibitions against torture and cruel treatment to relegate the use of so-called "enhanced interrogations" to the dustbin of history.

Enhanced Interrogation Is Simply Torture, American-Style

Hugh Gusterson

Hugh Gusterson is a professor of anthropology and international affairs at George Washington University. His expertise is in nuclear culture, international security, and the anthropology of science.

As an anthropologist, I am fascinated by the term "enhanced interrogation." It must surely take pride of place in the American lexicon of government euphemisms for violence, alongside such phrases from nuclear discourse as "collateral damage" (for the mass killing of civilians), "event" (for a nuclear explosion), "countervalue strike" (for the nuclear destruction of a city), "surgical strike" (a targeted strike with nuclear weapons), and "clean bombs" (nuclear weapons designed to optimize blast over radiation). As Carol Cohn notes in her classic article on the language of nuclear strategists, "Sex and Death in the Rational World of Defense Intellectuals," "'clean bombs' may provide the perfect metaphor for the language of defense analysts and arms controllers. This language has enormous destructive power, but without emotional fallout."

The same is true when it comes to "enhanced interrogation." My dictionary tells me that "to enhance" is to "improve in value, quality, desirability, or attractiveness." The word "enhanced" usually applies to images, food flavors, and consumer electronics, but why not torture as well? The rest of the world has classic torture, which involves electrodes, pincers, batons, and bloodstains. The United States, being exceptional, has enhanced torture, which involves rectal feeding (in other words, anal rape), no sleep for a week, "insult slaps," ice-cold baths, stress positions, being locked in a

"Torture, American-Style," by Hugh Gusterson, Bulletin of the Atomic Scientists, December 21, 2014. Reprinted by permission.

box for 18 hours, waterboarding, and threats that your mother's throat will be slit. But no bloodstains.

"Enhanced interrogation" is torture, American style. Exceptional torture. Torture that insists it is not torture. Post-torture? This uniquely American kind of torture has six defining characteristics.

First, it eschews tools used in medieval times or in Third World jails (with the exception of the centuries-old technique of waterboarding). If we are not using the classic tools of the torture trade—electrodes to the genitals, batons to the ribs—then, the theory goes, what we are doing cannot be torture. Above all, there must be no blood, burns, or scars, since these are the after signs of classic torture. American torture is cutting-edge and clean. It leaves no tell-tale marks.

Second, American torture techniques must be designed by scientific experts, so that they are certifiably modern, rational, and scientific. In this case the experts were the PhD psychologists James Mitchell and John Bruce Jessen, whose company was paid $81 million by US taxpayers to perfect the shiny new interrogation techniques.

Third, American torture is medically supervised. The Hippocratic oath to do no harm provides a fig leaf of immunity to the torturers, even if the CIA doctors who attended the torture sessions have been condemned by the American Medical Association for betraying their vocation. In a bizarre parsing of their conflicting obligations to the victims and their torturers, these doctors made sure that prisoners who underwent the agony of having their arms shackled for hours in painful positions were allowed to do so sitting down if they had broken bones in their feet, that prisoners' diets were adjusted so they would not permanently damage the esophagus when they vomited while being waterboarded, and that Tylenol was offered to alleviate the pain of torture.

Fourth, the fiction of legality must be maintained. No matter that the "black site" practice of establishing secret prisons in which to conduct torture clearly violated the Geneva Conventions and the Convention Against Torture (ratified by the United States in 1994) in most lawyers' opinions. Washington had to find lawyers who would certify that the new interrogation techniques did not constitute torture; the sheen of legality, no matter how risible, is vital. Thus John Yoo and James Bybee of the Office of Legal Counsel in the George W. Bush Justice Department certified that, as long as death or permanent organ damage did not result, it did not constitute torture to repeatedly bring a prisoner to the edge of death by drowning, shackle him in painful positions, deny him sleep for days at a time, or introduce foreign objects into his anus. The interrogators could then say they had it in writing that they were not torturers. Thus CIA official Jose Rodriguez told Fox News, "all of these techniques were approved by the lawyers." A tortured interpretation of the law trumps common sense.

Fifth, in keeping with American exceptionalism, the torture is presented as an exception, but one that proves the rule. "We don't torture," President George W. Bush said. "We don't torture people. OK?" said George Tenet, Bush's CIA director. That is the enunciation of the rule, the insistent proclamation of which coincides with its nullification in practice. Thus, while leaders tell us that the United States doesn't practice torture, apologists tell us that the days after the 9/11 attacks were a desperate time when "harsh measures" were, exceptionally, allowable to ensure there would be no more terrorist attacks. And, since 9/11, the United States has repeatedly invoked its status as the exceptional nation committed to human dignity and freedom to license offshore and black site suspensions of human dignity and freedom—a chain of suspensions that constitute an unacknowledged de facto reversal of the "we-do-not-torture" rule.

Finally, sixth, spin doctors are brought in to devise phrases like "enhanced interrogation," that, operating as phraseological cloud cover, obscure what lies beneath. "Enhanced interrogation" is a Madison Avenue term, like "new and improved," that seeks to make something seem more novel than it is while obscuring its defects. And, like all euphemisms, it dulls the spiritual pain of those whose job it is to inflict physical pain on others. It is a tool of what the anthropologist Didier Fassin calls "moral anesthesia." "Enhanced interrogation" is one of a whole new family of euphemistic phrases brought to us by the "war on terror"—a cousin to other sinisterly bland neologisms such as "unlawful combatant" (a guerilla out of uniform), "extraordinary rendition" (for illegal kidnapping by the state), and "signature strike" (for the deliberate killing by drone of people whose identity is unknown).

Whereas countries like Egypt and Myanmar leave torture to thugs who work over their victims' bodies in windowless cells, expecting news of their work to travel, the United States has brought in psychologists, doctors, lawyers, and spin doctors to rework it into torture bureaucratized to code, torture engineered for plausible deniability. This is torture, American style.

But euphemisms such as "enhanced interrogation" are also a symptom of repressed shame. The resort to euphemism betrays shame about that which cannot be honestly named. Now, finally, honesty is making a comeback. As more commentators and politicians openly use the old-fashioned word "torture," the hollowness of the euphemism becomes apparent, and it loses its power to obscure what was done in the CIA's hidden sites. Now "enhanced interrogation" increasingly finds itself in ironic quote marks, imparting a sense of rigidity and absurdism to the government spokespersons who insist on continuing to use it.

Reclaiming our language is the first step in confronting the crimes that were committed in our name. Let's stop using "enhanced interrogation," and, if Americans want to defend what their government did, at least call torture by its true name.

Many Coercive Techniques Are Not Torture

David B. Rivkin Jr.

David B. Rivkin Jr. is an attorney, political writer, and media commentator on issues of constitutional and international law, as well as foreign and defense policy. He defended former US defense secretary Donald Rumsfield against charges that an al-Qaeda operative was tortured while in US custody.

I t is always tough to balance liberty and public safety, even in peacetime. Balancing liberty and safety in wartime is the most difficult task, and certain aspects of wartime policies, like aggressive interrogation techniques, are hard to address, both emotionally and intellectually. The progress of civilization is such that we have all become kinder and more genteel about such issues and do not take well to any forms of government-sponsored coercion, whether physical or psychological. These are not pleasant issues but we do have to talk about them, if only to arrive at the right policy balance and satisfy ourselves as citizens that we are doing the right thing.

I largely agree with what my friend and colleague Will Taft had to say about the law, with a couple of caveats. First, with all due respect, the Supreme Court did not definitely establish that Common Article 3 applies to and binds the United States for all purposes. I submit that the Supreme Court cannot issue such sweeping pronouncements anyway, given the fairly narrow ways in which judicial power operates in our constitutional system. What the Supreme Court actually decided in *Hamdan* is that Common Article 3 applies to the particular set of issues before it; namely, the legality of the military commissions proposed by the president before the enactment of the Military Commissions Act. The Court

Excerpt from "Legal Standards and the Interrogation of Prisoners in the War on Terror," by Cynthia Arnson and Philippa Strum, Woodrow Wilson International Center for Scholars, December 2007. Reprinted by permission.

came to this decision through a very tidy trick; namely, by stating that Congress, in its infinite wisdom, did not give the president authority to create military commissions unsanctioned by "the laws of war," as codified by Congress in the Uniform Code of Military Justice, and rejecting the government's arguments that its Military Commissions procedures were authorized by statute.[1]

Congress incorporated Common Article 3 into the Uniform Code of Military Justice (UCMJ), a kind of omnibus legislation that deals with many issues of military discipline and order (an earlier version of the Code was called the Articles of War), by very obscure reference.[2] The UCMJ did no more than that. Moreover, it is not the province of the judiciary to make broad and sweeping statements about what international obligations have been assumed by the United States and how they are to be construed across the board, as distinct from the context of a particular case or controversy before the courts. That is important. However, the administration unfortunately threw in the towel on this issue. In my opinion, there is a perfectly defensible legal way to read the *Hamdan* opinion differently.

Will and I may also disagree somewhat about how clear words like "torture," "cruel," "inhumane" and "degrading" are as a matter of law, along with other language in Common Article 3 that refers to humiliation. I think that they are very capacious. That does not mean that they are completely devoid of meaning, but they are certainly not crystal clear, especially not in the context of criminal law enforcement, where one has to worry about such things as the legal doctrine that laws can be struck down as void for vagueness. Under our constitutional system, before one can prosecute people, one must spell out clearly the acceptable parameters of their conduct.

Some of those words are pretty clear; others are less so. I think the meaning of "torture" is more or less clear. I think the meaning of "cruel, inhumane and degrading" is less clear. With all due respect to those who claim otherwise, what "humiliation" means is utterly unclear, because it is driven by the cultural context. There are cultures where, because of fairly demeaning views of women, men find it humiliating to work for women. In many cultures, being interrogated by a woman or somebody, let us say, of Jewish faith, is extremely humiliating. I tend to doubt that most of you would feel that these sentiments, probably genuinely felt by individuals who espouse these views, should be indulged. If we were interrogating a neo-Nazi who had a fanatical hatred of Jews we would not remove everybody who is interrogating him, no matter how pleasantly and gently, who looks Jewish or in fact is Jewish. Humiliation is very culturally driven.

It is also context-driven. There are fundamental differences between civilian and military life. If I went back to my office, for example, and told my secretary or one of the more junior associates in my law firm to drop down and give me fifty pushups, I would be in trouble with my firm.

In military life, things have gotten a little kinder and gentler in basic and advanced training. The drill sergeants are not as tough and sadistic-sounding, but people still stand for a couple of hours at parade rest in full kit, which is a form of stress position. People are given 100 pushups or some such number. People must run with full gear, which is quite unpleasant and debilitating. Recruits experience being yelled at and told to scrub the floor with a toothbrush.

The whole essence of military life involves humiliating and degrading people, stripping away the soft layers of civilian identity and recasting them as warriors. I do not think many experts in military psychology and training would disagree with that. There is sleep deprivation and very bad nutrition; and, for those who go through more advanced training—pilots or Navy SEALs, for example—things that I don't think we've done to detainees, including the fact that some of our own people were waterboarded None of this is for sadistic purposes but, rather, to build resistance and to anticipate the possible use of those techniques by our enemies. You therefore have to understand the fundamental differences between the civilian and military spheres and realize that concepts like humiliation are context- and culture-specific.

It is also worth noting that there is plenty of coercion and humiliation in every criminal justice and penal system in the world, including even the most defendant-friendly systems like our own. In my view, being subjected to a custodial interrogation is inherently unpleasant and humiliating. You will have read stories about tough interrogators pressing detainees, and I am referring to not very sympathetic detainees, saying things like, "Look, unless you cooperate we're really going to go after your wife and she'll be in prison for the next fifteen years, but if you cooperate we'll cut her a deal and she's only going to do six years." I cannot imagine that this would not be extremely painful and very cruel from the perspective of the individual who is undergoing such an interrogation.

William Taft is correct that the old interrogation manual did not permit any discernable forms of coercion. That was a policy choice made by the United States. I see no evidence that the choice was made as a matter of law, after having analyzed the key legal strictures in international and domestic law. Frankly, since World War II and up until September 11, we were not very serious about unlawful combatants as a category. That does not mean, however, that we have given up the right to engage in conduct that is not prohibited, because customary international law changes in a rather glacier-like manner, and it requires more than a short-term absence of a given practice, before that practice becomes unavailable to a state.

An additional point about law is that the international law of war recognizes two categories of combatants, lawful and unlawful, and they receive vastly different privileges upon capture. Lawful combatants are honorable people, who upon capture should be treated with dignity, because all they have done is fight for their country or their cause, and they have simply suffered the misfortune of being caught. They are entitled to the gold standard level of treatment. They cannot be subjected to any humiliation. They cannot suffer any inducement to betray secrets; they have both the right and an obligation to protect their country's secrets. There can be no disadvantageous treatment of any kind.

Unlawful combatants are not entitled to receive anything approaching this gold standard level of treatment. They have to be treated humanely. They cannot be tortured. They cannot be subjected to cruel, inhumane and degrading treatment, but they can be interrogated aggressively. The question, again, is what constitutes an aggression.

Let me switch to some policy issues. Unfortunately, critics of our policies always use the "t" word, torture, to describe everything, but there are many unpleasant things that are not torture. People would not use words like cruel, inhumane, degrading, and humiliating if everything constituted torture. The use of the word torture has been cheapened in the sense that when everything is torture, nothing is torture.

I read statements by some of my European friends saying that the very fact that people are indefinitely in custody constitutes torture, because not knowing how long they will be there is a form of torture. With due respect, under that standard, every POW in every war has been tortured. I bet if you asked Winston Churchill, or a German POW in 1941, or an American or British POW following the Battle of Dunkirk, how long the war would last, he would not have been able to tell you. Those things are just unknowable. To call that torture is to devalue the word torture.

Now, is coercion necessary? We hear that if we are very clever, if we use the standard FBI techniques, if we appeal to people's good graces and talk about the fact that they are not going to see their families for a while and get into their psychological space, everything will be fine. I am not an interrogator. I have never been one, and I hope not to partake in this admittedly tough and unpleasant activity, but I will tell you one thing. In late 2001 and 2002, following our invasion of Afghanistan, we captured a number of al-Qaeda personnel. According to *The Washington Post, The New York Times* and various other newspapers that can hardly be accused of being sympathetic to the Bush administration, the

FBI was singularly unsuccessful in eliciting information from the detainees by using traditional FBI interrogation techniques. The reason the CIA swung into action and the debate arose in the administration about the definitional issues is because the other approaches did not work.

Some Israeli and British colleagues tell me that if you are really clever, if you know the language, if you know the culture of the people you capture, you can get most of the needed information out of people slowly and without any use of coercive techniques. They may be right, but I submit to you that we do not have that capability. Right now we certainly do not have many interrogators who are expert in the cultures of the regions from which most of the people we're fighting come. Using the culture is not an option. The discussion reminds me of debates in the Cold War days about defense procurements. Some people argued that because we had waste, fraud and mismanagement in the Defense Department—they were thinking of $900 toilet seats—we should not spend any money on defense until that was fixed. My answer at the time was no, that's not how you do things. You try to minimize waste, fraud and mismanagement, but in the interim you spend as many defense dollars as necessary to buy what you need. So, while there are undoubtedly some efficacious alternatives, I do not know how easily obtainable they are right now or will be in the foreseeable future. However, it is at least a debatable proposition.

What is not a debatable proposition is the claim that stress techniques do not work. I am really tired of hearing that because, if it were so, there would be no need to debate this admittedly unpleasant set of issues. Unfortunately, coercive techniques work, with all the caveats that William Taft mentioned. Yes, there is a small category of people who are so tough, so devout, so motivated that no matter what you do, you can literally pull them apart and they would not tell you anything. It is, however, a very small category.

Some of you may remember the movie *Marathon Man*. If you do not know anything, no matter how much you are tortured, you will not be able to tell anything. After a sadistic old Nazi-type drilled every single tooth Dustin Hoffman had to find out where the diamonds were hidden, he said, "I guess you really didn't know anything." But these are exceptions. I don't know what the statistical breakdown is but there are some people who will talk simply upon being captured. There is a fairly small category of people who will not talk no matter what you do to them. Then there is the vast middle of people who will talk if coercive techniques are applied.

I am also tired of hearing that people would lie if such techniques were used. Of course they would lie. If you capture people who want to fight to kill you, they would lie whether you interrogated them coercively or not. Unless you have the ability over time to cross-check what they tell you against what other people told you, and create a kind of mosaic-like complete intelligence picture, then interrogating people is useless. But if you do have enough time to cross-reference things, the fact that somebody lies is not a problem. In fact, once you figure out enough of a context, you can learn as much from the fact that somebody is lying to you as from somebody telling you the truth, as long as you are able to discern what is a lie and what is truth.

I do not know and I do not think any one of us knows how much intelligence we have gotten from people who were aggressively interrogated, but George Tenet, who certainly is not a big fan of this administration, has written that there were spectacular intelligence coups where information was obtained through aggressive interrogation techniques.[3] This has been mentioned by other people, including the President. The fact that as a general proposition throughout history, aggressive interrogation techniques have worked, suggests that it is a point worth exploring.

I will mention two other things briefly. First, I know there are people who chastise the administration for exercises like the John Yoo memo.[4] You may not like where he, the Office of Legal Counsel, the Department of Justice, and the White House counsels came out. There are some aspects of those memos with which I would not agree. What I ask you to appreciate, however, is how commendable it is that we, as a democratic society, faced with what was felt to be an extreme threat in the aftermath of September 11, actually asked legal questions. We wanted to understand not only what was right but what was legal. I would submit to you that most countries, including some of our democratic friends in Europe, would not have bothered asking legal questions. I doubt that the French Ministry of Defense or intelligence services obtained a legal opinion prior to having agents blow up the *Rainbow Warrior*, a ship protesting French nuclear tests in the Pacific, asking how they could avoid violating New Zealand law or international law. They just don't do those things. Their sense is that when you have something driven by *raison d'etat* you do what you have to do.

My bottom line on this issue is this. The legal matrix is not the driver as we address these questions. The laws, the Geneva Conventions, the torture conventions and such actually allow us more room for action. This is not a matter of a legal straitjacket but a policy-driven decision.

Finally, I am saddened by the fact that we as a body politic have not had a serious discussion about this in the last several years. We have had a lot of sloganeering. It does not take much courage to condemn torture and any inhumane or degrading treatment and all forms of coercions. If one wants to get confirmed by the Senate in the future, it is far safer to condemn all of that than to defend any aspect of coercion.

But by acting as if everything is torture, we fail to ask ourselves important questions. Are there degrees of coercion with which we as a society would be comfortable? I would submit to you that there should be at least some. I am not supportive of torture or cruel, inhumane, or degrading acts, but I find it difficult to imagine that we should not apply aggressive interrogation techniques—at least as aggressive as we use with regard to our own personnel—to unlawful enemy combatants. That would not include waterboarding, but it would include things like sensory deprivation, sleep deprivation, and moderate use of stress positions. I do not believe, if we do these things to our men and women who have joined up to wear a uniform, that we as a society should find it unacceptable to apply these techniques to unlawful enemy combatants. The notion that individuals volunteer for the armed services and are not prisoners is irrelevant because, as a matter of law, you cannot volunteer for things that are inherently illegal and against public policy. One cannot volunteer for prostitution; one cannot volunteer for torture. It is regrettable that we as a society have been unable at least to have a serious dialogue about these issues.

Notes

1. U.S. Department of Justice Office of Legal Counsel, Office of the Assistant Attorney General, "Memorandum for James B. Comey, RE: Legal Standards Applicable Under 18 U.S.C. 2340- 2340A," Dec. 30, 2004, available at news.findlaw.com/hdocs/docs/terrorism/dojtorture123004mem.pdf.

2. "Senate confirmation hearings for Alberto Gonzales, Senate Judiciary Committee Confirmation Hearing," Jan. 6, 2005, available at http://www.nytimes.com/2005/01/06/politics/ 06TEXT-GONZALES.html.

3. David Johnston, and James Risen, "Secret U.S. Endorsement Of Severe Interrogations," *The New York Times*, Oct. 4, 2007.

4. Eric Schmitt, "Army's New Rules Bar Harsh Interrogations," *International Herald Tribune*, Apr. 29, 2005.

Enhanced Interrogation Is Not "Plain-English" Torture

Marc A. Thiessen

Marc A. Thiessen is a columnist for the Washington Post *and a visiting fellow at the American Enterprise Institute. A former speechwriter for President George W. Bush and Secretary of Defense Donald Rumsfeld, he is the author of* Courting Disaster: How the CIA Kept America Safe and How Barack Obama Is Inviting the Next Attack.

New York Times executive editor Dean Baquet has declared the soon-to-be-released report on CIA interrogations prepared by Senate Intelligence Committee Democrats the "most definitive accounting of the program to date." Of course he has not read it. No one has. It's still classified. But why wait for the details? It comes to the right conclusions, from the Times' perspective, so let's declare it "definitive."

So convinced is Baquet by the report he has not read, that he recently announced that the Times will henceforth refer to the techniques used by the CIA as "torture." After all, President Obama recently declared that "we tortured some folks." And Obama *never* says *anything* that is untrue.

Baquet openly admits that both the Bush *and* Obama Justice Departments investigated and found the CIA had not violated US laws against torture. But, he says, there is a "specialized legal meaning" and a "plain–English" meaning of torture—and while the CIA interrogations did not meet the "legal meaning" they do meet this "plain–English" meaning.

When researching my book, "Courting Disaster," I interviewed some folks who understand the "plain–English" meaning of torture

"The New York Times and the 'Plain-English' Meaning of Torture," by Marc A. Thiessen, American Enterprise Institute, August 12, 2014. Reprinted by permission.

a heck of a lot better than the editors of the Times—American servicemen who suffered actual torture in North Vietnamese prison camps. Here is what these torture victims had to say about waterboarding.

Col. Bud Day, who passed away earlier this year, received the Medal of Honor for his heroic escape from a North Vietnamese prison camp. He suffered such excruciating torture at the hands of his captors that he became totally physically debilitated and unable to perform even the simplest task for himself. Here is what he told me about CIA waterboarding:

> I am a supporter of waterboarding. It is not torture. Torture is really hurting someone. Waterboarding is just scaring someone, with no long-term injurious effects. It is a scare tactic that works.

When I asked Day in an e-mail what he would say to the CIA officer who waterboarded Khalid Sheik Mohammed, Day replied immediately: "YOU DID THE RIGHT THING."

Col. Leo Thorsness also received the Medal of Honor for extraordinary heroism during the Vietnam War. During his captivity, his back was broken, and his body wrenched apart, by his North Vietnamese torturers. He says what the CIA did to al-Qaeda terrorists in its custody was not torture:

> To me, waterboarding is intensive interrogation. It is not torture. Torture involves extreme, brutal pain—breaking bones, passing out from pain, beatings so severe that blood spatters the walls … when you pop shoulders out of joints … In my mind, there's a difference, and in most POWs' minds there's a difference…. I would not hesitate a second to use 'enhanced interrogation,' including waterboarding, if it would save the lives of innocent people.

Another torture victim who supported waterboarding was the late Adm. Jeremiah Denton—the POW who famously winked the word "T-O-R-T-U-R-E" in Morse code during a North Vietnamese propaganda interview. Denton later received the Navy Cross for this courageous and costly act of defiance, for which he paid dearly when his captors figured out what he had done. I asked Denton if he thought waterboarding was torture. He told me:

> No, I think it's persuasive…. The big, monstrous difference here is that the gentlemen we are waterboarding are people who swore to kill Americans. They will wreak any kind of torture just for the hell of it on anybody. When they are captured by the US, and we know or have reason to believe that they know of a subsequent event after 9/11, if you don't interrogate them, more misery will take place…. Waterboarding is not an evil. Some of the things they did to us were torture. I passed out a dozen times from torture. We're not exerting that kind of excruciation.

But of course, what do these actual victims of torture know about torture? The Times says the CIA committed "torture." So, torture it is.

Here is a fact: more journalists have been waterboarded than terrorists. In undergoing the technique to see what it felt like, they were trying to prove waterboarding was torture. But they actually proved the opposite.

If someone had offered to attach electrodes to these journalists' bodies, and then flip the switch, do you think even one of them would have tried it to "see what it feels like"? How about having their nails ripped off with pliers? Or having their teeth drilled without anesthetic? Or being placed on a rack until their limbs popped out of their sockets? Or having screws attached to their legs, crushing their bones?

Not a chance. But they tried waterboarding.

So here is a "plain–English" definition of torture for The New York Times: if you are willing to try it to see what it feels like, *it's not torture.*

CHAPTER 4

Is Enhanced Interrogation Legal According to International Law?

Overview: The US Enhanced Interrogation Policy and the Geneva Conventions

Lionel Beehner

Lionel Beehner is assistant professor at the Modern War Institute at West Point. His work has been published in the Atlantic, Foreign Affairs, *the* New York Times, *the* Washington Post, *the* National Interest, *and the* New Republic, *among other publications.*

Introduction

A politically charged debate has roiled Congress in recent years over the torture and interrogation techniques of those detained by the United States. At issue is whether Central Intelligence Agency (CIA) officers who interrogate top terrorism suspects in detention centers abroad should be held accountable to the Geneva Conventions, which prohibits cruel and inhumane treatment of detainees. The White House wants to reinterpret the article to make it more specific and compliant with U.S. domestic law, specifically to prevent foreign detainees from suing CIA officers and other American officials for war crimes in international or domestic courts. The issue has exposed a rift between the White House and some prominent Republican lawmakers on Capitol Hill.

What Are the Geneva Conventions?

The Geneva Conventions provide an agreed-upon framework of legal protections to safeguard soldiers, civilians, and prisoners during wartime. The original Geneva Convention, drafted in 1864, dealt with the treatment of wounded troops. Shortly after the Second World War, it was expanded to include military personnel shipwrecked at sea, as well as prisoners of war and civilians under enemy control. The Conventions have been ratified by nearly every

"The United States and the Geneva Conventions," by Lionel Beehner, Council on Foreign Relations, September 20, 2006. Reprinted by permission.

country in the world—194 states in total—including the United States. Countries that violate the Geneva Conventions, including Common Article Three, can be held accountable for charges of war crimes.

What Is Common Article Three?

This article of the Geneva Conventions bars torture, cruel, inhumane, and degrading treatment, as well as outrages against the human dignity of prisoners of war, or POWs. Until recently it remained unclear whether the article applied to CIA interrogators, located overseas, who were questioning high-ranking members of al-Qaeda and other so-called "unlawful enemy combatants." In July 2006, the Supreme Court ruled in its *Hamdan* decision that this article does indeed apply to top terror suspects detained in CIA-run prisons as well as at Guantanamo Bay. "Quoting [Common Article Three] is like quoting the Bible for international lawyers," says Peter Danchin, a Columbia University legal expert.

Why Are the Geneva Conventions in the News?

Since September 11, 2001, the U.S. treatment of suspected terrorist detainees—both abroad and at Guantanamo Bay—has come under criticism from human rights groups and legal scholars. Writing in a January 2002 memo to President Bush, then White House Counsel Alberto Gonzales claimed clauses of the conventions referring to the detention and interrogation of enemy combatants were "obsolete." Bush, stretching back to 2002, has repeatedly declared detainees in U.S. custody should be treated "humanely, and to the extent appropriate and consistent with military necessity, in a manner consistent with the principles" of the Geneva Conventions. Yet critics of the Bush administration point to Abu Ghraib, the alleged abuses of Guantanamo Bay detainees, and the existence of CIA-run prisons overseas as evidence the Geneva Conventions have been not been enforced or followed.

What Is the White House's Position on the Geneva Conventions?

The White House has criticized the Supreme Court's *Hamdan* ruling for restricting its ability to prosecute and gather valuable intelligence from terrorist suspects overseas. "The administration has been compelled to act after *Hamdan* and the reaction from Congress," says Christopher Rassi, an associate legal officer for the UN International Criminal Tribunal for Rwanda. President Bush has called Common Article Three an unclear legal blueprint for interrogators. "The standards are so vague that our professionals won't be able to carry forward the program, because they don't want to be tried as war criminals. They don't want to break the law," he told reporters September 15. CIA officials, the *Wall Street Journal* reports, have begun taking out insurance policies that will cover civil judgments and legal costs if they are prosecuted.

President Bush, who says interrogations by CIA officials have prevented future terrorist attacks on U.S. soil, has proposed a bill that would, in effect, reinterpret Common Article Three to comport more with U.S. domestic law. Backers of the White House bill point to the issue of reciprocity, which forms part of the backbone of international law: States uphold international legal norms because they expect other states to do likewise. But because the enemy in the current context includes non-state actors like al-Qaeda or the Taliban, neither of which is expected to reciprocate and provide Geneva Conventions protections to U.S. detainees, the rules must be rewritten, they argue.

Why Are Some Republican Senators Opposed to this White House Bill?

Senators John McCain (R-AZ), John Warner (R-VA), and Lindsey Graham (R-SC) argue that a reinterpretation of the Geneva Conventions would put U.S. soldiers at risk abroad because it would allow other states to bend the rules. "What if a CIA paramilitary guy is caught in Iran," Graham told *Newsweek*. "What would our response be if the Iranian government put them on trial as a war criminal? We would scream bloody murder." Opponents of the White House bill also point to the moral authority of the United States in the war on terror. Rassi says the U.S. reinterpretation of the Geneva Conventions sets a bad precedent and could spark other states to follow suit, which undermines the effectiveness of these conventions.

Also at issue is the value of intelligence gleaned from torture or other forms of coercion. "Nothing is accomplished because it doesn't produce reliable testimony," says Linda Malone, a visiting professor at the University of Virginia Law School. "In fact, it actually does more damage than good." Opponents also question the value of military tribunals that allow hearsay testimony or evidence obtained from torture.

Why Do Some Military Officials Oppose the Bush Plan?

Legal experts say the Geneva Conventions had already been largely incorporated into the Pentagon's Uniform Code of Military Justice before revisions to the manual earlier this month banning specific forms of torture. "The definition of torture and of cruel and inhumane treatment has been workable from a military perspective [since the Second World War]," Malone says. "JAGs [Judge Advocate Generals] were saying they don't want it to be broken down into specifics." On September 13, a number of JAGs signed a letter in support of the White House bill, but experts say some of the uniformed lawyers were pressured to sign the statement and that many, in fact, objected to the Bush plan. "JAGs have said, 'We can do this [interrogate terrorist suspects] by following the rules,'" says David M. Crane, an international law professor at Syracuse University. "The wording of that letter [the JAGs signed] was like kissing your sister: supportive but with very faint praise."

Can the United States Technically Reinterpret Parts of the Geneva Conventions?

Only under U.S. domestic law, legal experts say. Signatories to treaties can attach reservations or include provisos at the time they sign or ratify international treaties. For example, the United States included a few reservations to the Geneva Conventions and their additional protocols on issues like the death penalty. However, it is uncommon for signatory states to revise their obligations many years after joining a treaty (of course, some states can choose to just opt out of treaties). In the case of the Geneva Conventions, "internationally this is settled black-letter law," Crane says. The issue, he says, focuses on a U.S. domestic debate to prevent foreign detainees from suing CIA officers for war crimes in U.S. domestic courts.

We Should Not Apply Human Rights Laws to Terrorists

Ted Lapkin

Ted Lapkin is the associate editor of the Review, *the monthly journal of the Australia/Israel and Jewish Affairs Council. His writing has appeared on the opinion pages of the* Los Angeles Times, *the* Washington Times, *the* Australian, *and the* Brisbane Courier-Mail.

From Manhattan to Mindanao, Islamist zealots draw no distinction between combatants and non-combatants. Jihadists target women, children, and the elderly without even the pretence of discrimination. In June 2004, an Al-Qaeda affiliated group distributed a video proudly documenting the beheading of a U.S. civilian, proclaiming: "the mujahedeen from the Fallujah Squadron slaughtered the American hostage Paul Johnson."[1] By spurning the laws of armed conflict, Islamist terrorists have created a conundrum for democracies: how do you fight people who throw the rulebook of warfare out the window?

Nazis and Islamists

The United States has faced such challenges before. In early morning darkness on June 13, 1942, a German U-boat surfaced off the coast of Long Island. Four men wearing German naval uniforms piled into a rubber dinghy and headed for shore. They buried their uniforms on the beach and headed toward their objective dressed in civilian clothes.[2] Four nights later, another German unit came ashore in northern Florida. After hitting the beach, they too discarded their uniforms.

These Nazi intelligence agents sought to sabotage targets

"Does Human Rights Law Apply to Terrorists?" by Ted Lapkin, the Middle East Forum, 2004. PP. 3-13. http://www.meforum.org/651/does-human-rights-law-apply-to-terrorists. Reprinted by permission.

within the United States. They were unsuccessful. Several weeks later, the Federal Bureau of Investigation (FBI) arrested them in Chicago and New York, remanding them to a U.S. army military commission for trial.

Like the "illegal combatants" held today at the U.S. naval base in Guantánamo Bay, Cuba, these Nazi saboteurs challenged the legality of the military tribunal process. Their lawyers took the case all the way to the Supreme Court, which ruled against them. In a unanimous decision delivered by Chief Justice Harlan Fiske Stone, the court determined that the German agents had violated the law of war and that a "military commission was lawfully constituted" to try them for that crime. Thus, declared the Supreme Court, "the motions for leave to file petitions for writs of habeas corpus are denied."[3]

Fast-forward almost sixty years. Foreign agents infiltrate the United States. Again, they don civilian clothes to cloak their operations. Nineteen hijackers board aircraft in Washington and Boston, seize them, and crash them into the World Trade Center, the Pentagon, and a field in rural Pennsylvania. On September 20, 2001, President George W. Bush stood before a joint session of Congress and declared war against terrorism, "Tonight we are a country awakened to danger and called to defend freedom … Whether we bring our enemies to justice, or bring justice to our enemies, justice will be done."[4]

The world did not have to wait long to see Bush back his rhetoric with action. Less than three weeks later, U.S. forces invaded Afghanistan to destroy the Taliban and Al-Qaeda's sanctuary. While fighting, U.S. troops encountered foreigners who had cast their lot with Osama bin Laden. The ranks of these jihadists included Western converts to Islam such as American John Walker Lind and Australian David Hicks. They also seized immigrant nationals or their children from Canada, Belgium, Denmark, France, Russia, Spain, Sweden, as well as many Muslim nations. These jihadists neither wore uniforms, nor respected the Geneva Conventions. On March 4, 2002, for example, an unmanned reconnaissance aircraft captured on film the summary execution of captured 32-year-old Navy SEAL Neil Roberts by three jihadists.[5] Accordingly, the United States made a decision to detain these captured Al-Qaeda and Taliban fighters as illegal combatants, rather than prisoners of war.

International law has progressed in the six decades since the Supreme Court ruled against the Nazi saboteurs. But, despite the arguments made by numerous academics and human rights activists, the law does not necessarily side with the detainees. In its 2004 *Rasul v. Bush* decision, the U.S. Supreme Court upheld the right of the U.S. government to detain enemy combatants, even if they are American citizens. The court, however, mandated that non-American detainees could challenge their incarceration in U.S. courts.[6]

The question of how to treat captured jihadists extends beyond Guantánamo Bay, Afghanistan, and Iraq: Israel has for years been forced to contend with Palestinian terrorist organizations that dispatch suicide bombers. Both the Kurdistan Workers Party (Partiya Karkaren Kurdistan, PKK) and various Islamist groups target Turkish civilians.

But, while the human rights community has been critical of certain United States policies for years, since September 11, the Bush administration has matched or perhaps even surpassed Israel and Turkey as a primary target of such groups as Amnesty International and Human Rights Watch.

Many nongovernmental organizations reserve venom for their condemnation of the U.S. policy of detaining captured Al-Qaeda and Taliban fighters as illegal combatants. Amnesty International labels the U.S. detention facility at Guantánamo Bay a "human rights scandal."[7] Both Amnesty International and Human Rights Watch condemn Washington's characterization of captured jihadists as illegal combatants as a violation of the Geneva Conventions. "In its treatment of the detainees at Guantánamo," declared Human Rights Watch, the United States "has been unwilling to fully apply international humanitarian law... [and] has flouted international human rights standards."[8] Amnesty International has adopted a similarly critical attitude. In a statement to the sixtieth session of the U.N. Human Rights Commission, Amnesty referred to "the human rights scandal of Guantánamo Bay" where "international law was flouted from the outset."[9]

Who Do the Geneva Conventions Protect?

But to what extent do the laws of armed conflict really apply in the war against terror? The answer resides primarily in the text of the 1949 Third Geneva Convention,[10] intended to ensure humane treatment for captured legal combatants. The International Committee of the Red Cross (ICRC) declared the Geneva Conventions to be the "bedrock of principles and rules that must guide the conduct of hostilities and the treatment of persons who have fallen into the hands of a party to an armed conflict."[11] The Red Cross has gone so far as to demand mandatory application of the Geneva Conventions "wherever a situation of violence reaches the level of an armed conflict."[12]

Yet, treaties are more like commercial contracts in that they are traditionally viewed as binding only among their parties. Some multinational agreements have evolved into the universally applicable "customary international law." This development is enshrined in the doctrine of *jus cogens*, which asserts the existence of a higher law that supersedes both national law and international agreements.[13]

In the wake of World War II, the international military tribunal at Nuremburg declared that the 1907 Hague Regulations Respecting the Laws and Customs of War on Land to be customary international law.[14] Yet, jurists have reached no such consensus about whether the 1949 Geneva Conventions have made such a transition.[15]

Unfortunately, the basis for the Red Cross's conclusion appears to have more to do with institutional self-aggrandizement than with international law. Many leftist academics and activists insist that the Geneva Conventions must be universally applied. Yet, that argument is undercut by those treaties' texts. The Third Geneva

Convention explicitly states that parties need not apply it to all conflicts, especially when the foes are not parties, and when enemies do not abide by its terms.[16]

No terrorist group is a party to the Geneva Conventions. They have not signed, much less ratified, those treaties. Moreover, it is evident that Hamas, Hezbollah, and members of the global Al-Qaeda network spurn both the spirit and the letter of international treaties designed to ameliorate the cruelty of war. Bloody attacks in New York, Jerusalem, Bali, Madrid, and Beslan are testament to the fact that these groups seek to kill civilians rather than to take captives. And when Islamist terrorists do seize hostages, brutality rather than protection appears to be the rule.

Iraqi insurgents beheaded 26-year-old American businessman Nicholas Berg and shot 20-year-old Keith Matthew Maupin shortly after the June 28, 2004 transfer of sovereignty. On July 22, Iraqi police found the beheaded corpse of a Bulgarian hostage. The Arabic satellite television network Al-Jazeera had confirmed on July 13 that it had a tape showing his execution.[17] Iraqi captors have also executed Pakistanis, a Turk, and a South Korean, among others. Such mistreatment of prisoners is not a new phenomenon among terrorist groups. In the 1980s, Hezbollah captured a number of Westerners in Lebanon, among them priests, journalists, professors, a librarian, and even the president of the American University of Beirut. Hezbollah tortured and hanged U.S. Marine lieutenant colonel William Higgins. Iraqi insurgents who decapitate civilian hostages have no more international legal claim to protection than did Hezbollah kidnappers.

By violating every tenet of international law regarding treatment of prisoners, terrorist groups forfeit any entitlement to protection under the Geneva Conventions. U.S. forces would be within their legal rights to treat captured Al-Qaeda members as they did Nazi saboteurs during World War II—trial by military commission and execution by firing squad.[18]

A similar argument applies to the Taliban. In 1956, the government of Afghanistan signed the Geneva Conventions.

If the Taliban were the legitimate government of Afghanistan, then the United States would be bound to apply the Third Geneva Convention to captured Taliban fighters. Yet, only three governments—Pakistan, Saudi Arabia, and the United Arab Emirates—recognized the Taliban's claim to power. In fact, throughout this period, the rival Northern Alliance occupied Afghanistan's seat at the United Nations. A typical illustration of the U.N.'s noncommittal attitude towards the Taliban appears in U.N. Security Council Resolution 1267 which addressed the group as only an "Afghan faction."[19] After a fistfight erupted between diplomats at the Afghan embassy in Washington, police simply expelled everyone and shuttered the building.

If international bodies did not recognize the Taliban as Afghanistan's legitimate government, then their militias could not be considered Afghanistan's regular armed forces any more than Hezbollah can be considered the army of Lebanon. Thus, Taliban fighters were not eligible for automatic Third Geneva Convention coverage. The United States is simply not obligated to extend Third Geneva Convention protections to every militia or organization that has pretensions to power.

A subsection of article four does afford automatic prisoner of war (POW) privileges to "members of regular armed forces who profess allegiance to a government or authority not recognized by the detaining power."[20] Accordingly, even if Washington did not recognize the authority of Mullah Omar's regime, U.S. forces would still be obligated to grant POW status to the Taliban had the Taliban been a regular force. But, the Taliban was anything but a regular force. Secretary of Defense Donald Rumsfeld addressed this issue at a February 8, 2002 press conference:

> The Taliban did not wear distinctive signs, insignias, symbols or uniforms … To the contrary, far from seeking to distinguish themselves from the civilian population of Afghanistan, they sought to blend in with civilian non-combatants, hiding in mosques and populated areas. They [were] not organized in military units, as such, with identifiable chains of command….[21]

Does International Law Protect Terrorists?

Some pundits and journalists condemn U.S. policy as a flagrant violation of the Geneva Conventions. Writing in the *Guardian*, a left-wing British broadsheet, professor of human rights law Conor Gearty proclaimed U.S. policy to be "cruel, unnecessary and as dangerous now as it was when first introduced."[22] But Gearty's criticism is more emotional than substantive. Nothing in the conventions requires that all captives receive prisoner of war status. In fact, article four of the Third Geneva Convention stipulates a number of requirements that must be met before a captive irregular combatant can qualify as a prisoner of war.

The drafters of the 1949 Geneva Conventions sought to base the treaty on past precedent. While the 1907 Hague regulations stipulated that "the laws, rights, and duties of war apply not only to armies, but also to militia and volunteer corps," those same regulations also presented a four-part test to determine eligibility of those irregular forces for lawful combatant status.[23] In order to be recognized as legitimate combatants, the Hague regulations required irregular units to "be commanded by a person responsible for his subordinates; to have a fixed distinctive emblem recognizable at a distance; to carry arms openly; and to conduct their operations in accordance with the laws and customs of war."[24]

The drafters of the Third Geneva Convention adopted this four-part test as part of the criteria to determine eligibility for POW status. The delegates drafting the convention made quite clear in their debates that they did not want to confer automatic POW status on irregular forces. After much negotiation, a special committee of the conference resolved this question by crafting article 4(A) so as to differentiate between regular armed forces, constituent volunteer corps, and militias on one hand, from irregular resistance movements, on the other. The drafters agreed to apply the Hague four-part test to the latter.[25]

Terrorists groups ranging from separatists like the PKK in Turkey, Chechen rebels in Russia, or the Pakistani-backed Harakat ul-Mujahideen in India; to Palestinian groups like Hamas,

Palestinian Islamic Jihad, and the Al-Aqsa Martyrs' Brigade, to the numerous cells that comprise the Al-Qaeda network all fail the four-part test. Hijacking civilian airliners and flying them into office buildings is not "in accordance with the laws and customs of war," nor is using human bombs to blow up buses, nor is lining up and executing school teachers. On these grounds, as well, the Taliban also forfeited claim to POW status. While they did carry arms openly, they neither observed the international humanitarian law, nor wore any recognizable sign to distinguish themselves from civilians.[26]

During the chaos of combat, confusion often reigns supreme. In battlefield confusion, captured combatants' eligibility for POW status may not be clear. During the mid-1980s, I served in Lebanon as an officer in Israel's Golani infantry brigade. We were engaged in a classic guerrilla war against Hezbollah, Amal, and Palestinian fighters who dressed in blue jeans and toted RPG-7s and AK-47s. At the slightest hint of disadvantage, these combatants would drop their weapons and melt away into the nearest Lebanese village, where they would try to blend into the local population.

The ensuing murkiness is precisely why the Third Geneva Convention demands that a "competent tribunal" determine the status of prisoners where there is doubt as to their proper status.[27] But, while it mandates that a tribunal be held, the convention does not dictate details of the process.

In its war against terror, the U.S. military adheres to the competent tribunal requirement. No detainee ended up in Guantánamo without a series of interrogations by U.S. intelligence officials. This process was intended to determine whether a prisoner was a bona fide enemy or an innocent bystander in the wrong place at the wrong time. Questions were asked, explanations given, and evaluations made. Thus, while Australian jihadist David Hicks wound up in Guantánamo and will shortly appear before a U.S. military commission, Afghan Haji Faiz Muhammad was arrested on suspicion of affiliation with the Taliban and was later released. Faiz Muhammad had few complaints about his treatment in U.S.

custody, declaring "we had enough food to eat. We could pray and wash with water five times a day."[28]

Facilitating the Fight against Al-Qaeda

Despite being under no legal obligation to do so, the U.S. government treats the Guantánamo detainees in a manner consistent with the Third Geneva Convention. Why does Washington apply the letter and not the spirit of the Third Geneva Convention to the Guantánamo detainees? In principle, the Bush administration believes that members of an enemy organization that flies hijacked airliners into office buildings should not be rewarded for their crimes.[29] The privileges of Geneva Convention status are simply that—privileges. Moreover, in practice, the ability to circumvent the Geneva Conventions gives U.S. forces a substantial advantage in prosecuting its war against Al-Qaeda and other terrorist proxies.

This would allow more intrusive questioning for captured terrorists than the Geneva Conventions permits for prisoners of war. But, that does not make U.S. actions illegal or mean that the United States is guilty of torture, as some human rights activists have claimed.[30] The U.N. Convention against Torture and Other Cruel, Inhuman, or Degrading Treatment or Punishment (UNCAT) defines torture as "any act by which severe pain or suffering, whether physical or mental, is intentionally inflicted on a person."[31]

But, it is doubtful whether sleep deprivation or sensory disorientation constitutes "severe pain or suffering." While all four Geneva Conventions contain a common article three containing an injunction against, "cruel treatment and torture,"[32] the interpretation of this provision rests upon the definition of torture for which the definitive document is the U.N. torture convention. True, Article 16 of UNCAT states, "Each State Party shall undertake to prevent in any territory under its jurisdiction other acts of cruel, inhuman or degrading treatment or punishment which do not amount to torture." But, international legal language is precise. Obligation to "undertake to prevent" is not absolute prohibition. While lesser categories of coercion should not be routine, they may be available to intelligence authorities in the event of a classic ticking bomb scenario. Can some degree of force be used, for example, on a terrorist who has knowledge of an impending attack? If depriving a captured Al-Qaeda operative of sleep could prevent a bombing such as that which struck Madrid in March 2004, would that be a greater violation of international law than allowing the slaughter of innocents to proceed?

The U.S. government is not only within its rights but is also wise to hold Al-Qaeda members incommunicado. A prisoner's military value does not solely consist of the information that a captive carries in his head. By holding Al-Qaeda members incommunicado, the U.S. military can sow the seeds of confusion and uncertainty in terrorist ranks. If bin Laden's followers do not know whether one of their comrades has been captured, then they also do not know whether any of their operations have been compromised. This is at the heart of the controversy about whether U.S. officials prematurely revealed that they had captured an Al-Qaeda computer specialist named Muhammad Naim Nur Khan who had assisted authorities in entrapping other Al-Qaeda operatives who were unaware of his capture.[33] Yet, if the Third Geneva Convention were applied to terrorists, the treaty's strict rules on reporting the capture of enemy POWs would make such a ruse *de guerre* impossible and would lead to the death of more civilians.

Thus, U.S. policy in its war against terror is consistent with the Third Geneva Convention. But, human rights advocates, such as Anthony Dworkin of the Crimes of War Project, argue that U.S. detention of suspected Al-Qaeda fighters in Afghanistan or suspected insurgents in Iraq nonetheless violates the Fourth Geneva Convention Relative to the Protection of Civilian Persons in Time of War.[34] The terms of this convention are expansive and seek to prevent unnecessary hardship to civilians in occupied territory. Nevertheless, any argument that U.S. policy violates the Fourth Geneva Convention can only be based on a very selective reading of that treaty. After all, regardless of how ambitious the convention's terms are, they still recognize the exigencies of war and the necessity to govern captured territory. The convention, for example, allows combatants to deny protections to an occupied territory's residents if those residents threaten security.[35] Thus, when the United States and Great Britain accepted formal occupying power status in Iraq under the terms of U.N. Security Council Resolution 1483, the international community gave them the ability to detain civilians for the overall security of coalition troops.

Israel, too, as an occupying power, has every legal right to pursue Palestinian terrorists and detain Palestinian civilians in the West Bank and Gaza. And, while these detentions cannot be open-ended, provisions to release terrorist suspects "at the earliest date consistent with the security of the State or Occupying Power" are open to interpretation. When car bombs target Iraqi civilians and politicians on the streets of Baghdad, and when suicide bombers attack Israeli buses on the streets of Jerusalem, neither U.S. nor Israeli authorities are under any obligation to release detainees. When push comes to shove, drafters of the convention recognized that the demands of legitimate military necessity always trump the extension of the treaty's privileges.

Human rights organizations and activists have also demanded that the U.S. government apply the International Covenant on Civil and Political Rights (ICCPR) to Guantánamo detainees. According to Amnesty International, U.S. detention of illegal combatants violates ICCPR clauses against arbitrary arrest or detention.[36] This is disingenuous, however, since the ICCPR also contains a clause that permits governments to suspend its application:

> In time of public emergency which threatens the life of the nation and the existence of which is officially proclaimed, the States [and] Parties to the present Covenant may take measures derogating from their obligations under the present Covenant to the extent strictly required by the exigencies of the situation, provided that such measures are not inconsistent with their other obligations under international law and do not involve

discrimination solely on the ground of race, color, sex, language, religion or social origin.[37]

On November 13, 2001, President Bush promulgated a military order entitled, "Detention, Treatment, and Trial of Certain Non-Citizens in the War against Terrorism." This presidential directive declared that the attacks of September 11, 2001, were "on a scale that has created a state of armed conflict that requires the use of the United States Armed Forces." The order went on to "proclaim a national emergency" in order to prevent terrorists from inflicting "mass deaths, mass injuries, and massive destruction of property" which could "place at risk the continuity of the operations of the United States Government."[38]

The Bush administration has carefully positioned itself within the bounds of international law. Bush's proclamation satisfied both the procedural and substantive prerequisites for suspending the arbitrary arrest clauses of the ICCPR. Human rights advocacy groups may not like it, but international law is not always consistent with their political agendas.

Do Human Rights Groups Undermine International Law?

During the past century and a half, the world has witnessed almost 100 attempts to implement international agreements that would constrain the violence of war.[39] While many, if not most, of those conventions have fallen by the wayside through general disregard, a few have served to ameliorate the suffering caused by armed conflicts. What separated relevant from irrelevant agreements was pragmatism.

The authors of the 1949 Geneva Conventions were realists who recognized that by attempting to ban everything, they would stop nothing.

Distinction between permissible and impermissible violence is the keystone of international humanitarian law. The international consensus that certain weapons and tactics should be outlawed depends upon this distinction. Chemical weapons, for example, are clearly illegal. The practical implementation of the rules depends upon soldiers' ability to discriminate between what is military and what is not. In the words of an International Committee of the Red Cross educational pamphlet, "It is a basic principle of international humanitarian law that persons fighting in armed conflict must, at all times, distinguish between civilians and combatants and between civilian objects and military objectives."[40]

Anything that obscures the distinction between combatant and noncombatant undermines the entire foundation of international humanitarian law. Any erosion in the ability to differentiate between civilians and soldiers on the battlefield inevitably would automatically place noncombatants at greater risk. If soldiers are distinctively marked or uniformed, then troops are less likely to mistake civilians for armed combatants and fire upon them. Yet, by seeking to ban detention of illegal combatants in facilities like Guantánamo Bay, this is precisely where the recommendations of the human rights industry would lead.

Political corruption of international law is a serious issue. The U.N. Human Rights Commission, especially under the tenure of Mary Robinson, placed politics over sound legal principle. It is precisely because international jurists and human rights experts remain unaccountable and free to pursue political agendas that the U.S. government has remained vigilant.

The Protocol Additional to the Geneva Convention provides a textbook example of the dangers of such ideological pollution. Drafted at the height of the Cold War, the Soviet bloc and its Third World allies sought recognition for those who fight "against colonial domination and alien occupation and against racist regimes."[41] But, the most perniciously politicized provisions of the protocol appear in article 44, which bestows automatic POW status on all combatants, including so-called freedom fighters, even if they violate the laws of war.[42] Another clause would permit fighters to retain legal combatant status even if they fight in civilian clothes.[43] Thus, in one fell swoop, the drafters struck a body blow against the entire system of international humanitarian law. Not only did the Soviet sphere try to emasculate any incentive for combatants to abide by the law of war, but they also sought to obfuscate the vital distinction between combatants and noncombatants.

While the Carter administration signed the 1977 Geneva Protocol, the Reagan administration understood the damage the treaty would do. Because of the drafters' overt political agenda, the United States declined to become party to the additional protocol.[44] The Bush administration is fortunate that the Senate did not ratify the treaty. Had it done so, captured Al-Qaeda terrorists could shield themselves with the very same civilized guidelines that they hold in such contempt.

Many academics, pundits, and politicians have sought to transform the Geneva Conventions into something they are not. The fundamental violations of international law committed by terrorists, be they in Afghanistan, Iraq, Israel, Spain, or Russia, render them ineligible for Geneva Convention protection. To apply the Geneva Conventions universally would be the undoing of those treaties. If there is no price to pay for doffing their uniform or shuttling combatants in Red Crescent ambulances, then soldiers would figure such illegalities to be worth it. Serious violations of the laws of war would become the equivalent of jaywalking. Those advocating universal application of the Geneva Conventions to detainees in Guantánamo Bay are, in effect, encouraging future combatants to transform hospitals into ammunition depots and schools into machine gun nests. The entire regime of international humanitarian law would crumble, and the protections it provides to noncombatants in war would disappear.

The laws of war are imperfect instruments, often "more honored in the breach than the observance."[45] Yet, despite their inherent limitations, they are humanity's best chance to restrain the savagery of war. The key to their effectiveness—and the ability of Western democracies to fight terrorism—lies in their ability to establish a clear differentiation between licit and illicit means of conducting armed conflict. To blur this distinction and to unnecessarily apply the Geneva Conventions to illegal combatants would erode that distinction and constitute not only a legal mistake, but an ethical one as well.

Notes

1. CNN.com, June 19, 2004, at http://www.cnn.com/2004/WORLD/meast/06/18/ saudi.kidnap/.

2. Ex Parte Quirin, 317 US 1 (1942), U.S. Supreme Court, at http://www.law.umkc. edu/faculty/projects/ftrials/conlaw/quirin.html.

3. Ibid.

4. Address to a joint session of Congress, United States Capitol, Washington, D.C., at http://www.whitehouse.gov/news/releases/2001/09/20010920-8.html.

5. BBC.com, Mar. 6, 2002, at http://news.bbc.co.uk/1/hi/world/south_asia/1857599. stm.

6. Rasul v Bush (03-334) 321 F.3d 1134, reversed and remanded.

7. "Guantánamo Bay: A Human Rights Scandal," Amnesty International, at http:// web.amnesty.org/pages/guantanamobay-index-eng.

8. "United States: Guantánamo Two Years On," Human Rights Watch, Jan. 9, 2004, at http://www.hrw.org/english/docs/2004/01/09/usdom6917.htm.

9. "The Human Rights Scandal of Guantanamo Bay," Amnesty International, AI Index: IOR 41/024/2004, no. 098, Apr. 20, 2004.

10. Geneva Convention (III) Relative to the Treatment of Prisoners of War, at http://www.icrc.org/ihl. nsf/7c4d08d9b287a42141256739003e636b /6fef854a3517b75ac125641e004a9e68?OpenDocument.

11. "International Law and the Challenge of Armed Conflicts," 28th International Conference of the Red Cross and Red Crescent, Dec. 2-6, 2003, p. 5.

12. Ibid., p. 8.

13. The Vienna Convention on the Law of Treaties, 1969, 1155 UNTS 331, art. 53, at http://www.un.org/law/ilc/texts/treaties.htm.

14. "Judgment of the International Military Tribunal of Nuremberg," Sept. 30 and Oct. 1, 1946, p. 65.

15. Yoram Dinstein, "Application of Customary International Law," in Michael Bothe, ed., National Implementation of International Humanitarian Law: Proceedings of an International Colloquium Held at Bad Homburg, June 17-19, 1988 (Leiden: Brill Academic Publishers, 1991), p. 31.

16. Geneva Convention (III), art. II, para. 3.

17. CNN.com, July 13, 2004, at http://www.cnn.com/2004/WORLD/meast/07/13/ iraq.main/.

18. Ex Parte Quirin, 317 U.S. 1 (1942).

19. Text at http://www.state.gov/s/ct/rls/other/5110.htm.

20. Geneva Convention (III), art. 4(A)3.

21. Donald H. Rumsfeld, U.S. Department of Defense news conference, Feb. 8, 2002, at http://usinfo.org/usia/usinfo.state.gov/topical/pol/terror/02020818.htm.

22. The Guardian (London), July 7, 2004.

23. Final Record of the Diplomatic Conference of Geneva of 1949, Federal Political Department, Bern, p. 467.

24. Convention (IV) respecting the Laws and Customs of War on Land and its Annex: Regulations Concerning the Laws and Customs of War on Land, Hague, 18 October 1907, at http://www.icrc.org/ihl. nsf/0/1d1726425f6955aec125641e0038bfd6?OpenDocument.

25. Final Record of the Diplomatic Conference of Geneva of 1949, p. 422.

26. Rumsfeld, news conference, Feb. 8, 2002.

27. Geneva Convention (III), art. 5, para. 2.

28. BBC News World Edition, Oct. 29, 2002, at http://news.bbc.co.uk/2/hi/south_asia/2371349.stm.

29. Theodore B. Olsen, solicitor general of the United States, "Brief for the Respondents," Rasul v Bush (03-334) 321 F.3d 1134, reversed and remanded.

30. U.S.-based Australian lawyer Richard Bourke claimed that Australian Guantánamo detainees David Hicks and Mamdouh Habib were being tortured. Radio National PM, Australian Broadcasting Corporation, Oct. 8, 2003.

31. Text at http://www.unhchr.ch/html/menu3/b/h_cat39.htm.

32. Geneva Conventions I, II, III, IV, art. 3-1A, at http://www.icrc.org/ihl.nsf/ WebCONVFULL?OpenView.

33. Associated Press, Aug. 9, 2004.

34. Anthony Dworkin, "America's Interrogation Network: Rules on the Treatment of Prisoners in International Law," Crimes of War Project, at http://www. crimesofwar.org/onnews/news-prison2.html.

35. Convention (IV) relative to the Protection of Civilian Persons in Time of War, Geneva, 12 August 1949, art. 5, para. 1, at http:// www.icrc.org/ihl.nsf/7c4d08d9b287a42141256739003e636b/ 6756482d86146898c125641e004aa3c5?OpenDocument.

36. "USA: Guantánamo Detainees—The Legal Black Hole Deepens," Amnesty International, Mar. 12, 2003.

37. International Covenant on Civil and Political Rights, 1966, part 2, art. 4, at http:// www.mediator.online.bg/eng/iccpr-2.htm.

38. White House news release, Nov. 13, 2001, at http://www.state.gov/coalition/cr/ prs/6077.htm.

39. "States Parties & Signatories, by Treaties," ICRC, at http://www.icrc.org/ihl.nsf/ WebNORM?OpenView.

40. "International Humanitarian Law and Terrorism: Questions and Answers," ICRC, May 2004, at http://www.icrc.org/Web/eng/siteeng0.nsf/html/5YNLEV.

41. Protocol Additional to the Geneva Conventions of 12 August 1949, and Relating to the Protection of Victims of International Armed Conflicts (Protocol 1), art. 1, sec. 4, at http://www.icrc.org/ihl.nsf/7c4d08d9b287a42141256739003e636b/ f6c8b9fee14a77fdc125641e0052b079?OpenDocument.

42. Ibid., art. 44, sec. 2.

43. Ibid., art. 44, sec. 3.

44. "Letter of Transmittal from President Ronald Reagan to the United States Senate, 29 January 1989," reprinted in American Journal of International Law, vol. 81, no. 4, p. 910.

45. William Shakespeare, Hamlet, act 1, scene 4.

The United States Had Legal Authority to Use Enhanced Interrogation

John A. Rizzo

John A. Rizzo was a lawyer in the Central Intelligence Agency for many years. He was the deputy counsel or acting general counsel of the CIA for the first nine years of the war on terror, during which the CIA used enhanced interrogation techniques on detainees. He is a visiting fellow at the Hoover Institution and senior counsel at the Steptoe and Johnson law firm.

A 34-year agency veteran, [John] Rizzo has been described as "the most influential career lawyer in CIA history." He was the agency's acting general counsel during the implementation of its controversial "enhanced interrogation" program, which he says the CIA undertook because "measures like this were the only possible effective way to glean" critical intelligence from high-value detainees. Though he says the program was necessary and effective, one "major mistake" he believes the CIA made was not briefing more members of Congress about it. This is [an excerpt of] the edited transcript of an interview conducted on Sept. 8, 2011.

You went down to Guantanamo in September of 2002. What was the purpose of that trip?
I went down with a number of the other senior lawyers in the government involved in detention and interrogation matters. It was organized by the general counsel of the Department of Defense. My purpose in going was simply to acclimate myself with Guantanamo, the facilities. We did have a presence there because we [were]

analyzing the intelligence that the Guantanamo detainees were providing to their military trainers.

But you weren't conducting interrogations there?
We were not.

And the other members of that team were looking at just what interrogation techniques could be sanctioned?
Well, I can't speak for them entirely. But frankly, that was not my impression at the time. I think most of them were there for the same reason I was, just [to] look at the facility and the housing and to also talk to the people, the U.S. government officials, who were assigned there.

So at that point, decisions had already been taken as to just what interrogation techniques would be allowed?
Well, the decisions about CIA, yes.

That process that you went through, but also what techniques the military, the joint task force could undertake?
I was generally aware of those. I knew those discussions were going on.

One gets the impression that those secret detention facilities overseas where people were rendered, you had more legal cover to do things there than you could do at Guantanamo.
We certainly had what I thought at the time was explicit, definitive legal authority to engage in a given set of specific techniques.

Up to waterboarding?
Up through waterboarding, yes.

Beyond waterboarding?
Well, depends on where one places the scale of seriousness of these techniques. Certainly including waterboarding.

Again, my job was to oversee the CIA legal compliance and its interrogation practices. I was aware there were discussions going on between the Department of Defense, the Department of Justice. I was aware that the Department of Defense and the military were drawing up lists of techniques. But to tell you the truth, I wasn't mixing and matching.

Just as an observer, you're in the loop on all of this; you're talking to the other lawyers in the other departments, I assume. Were you aware of the tensions between the FBI and the Department of Defense over interrogations at Guantanamo?
You know, I met regularly with the general counsel [for] the Department of Defense on a weekly basis—

Was it [William J.] Haynes?
He wasn't a good friend. I seem to recall him mentioning that there were certainly ongoing disputes about treatment of Guantanamo prisoners between FBI and DoD officials—

You knew from the Department of Defense that they were getting pushback from the FBI over what was going on with the detainees?
I was aware that there were differences of opinion about treatment standards for questioning detainees, but I didn't know much beyond that.

This one case of the reports that came out, [Mohammed al-] Qahtani, is asked to stand nude in front of a female guard; insults are hurled at him about his mother and his sister. What's your opinion about these?
Well, I thought they were clearly excessive. There was certainly nothing along those lines was ever sought by CIA for authority.

I believe there was an issue about the use of dogs at Guantanamo. Thanks to the new Obama administration, the world can see exactly which techniques we propose to use and which techniques we did use. And that was it.

So that information getting out about how he was treated was not a window on the kinds of things that were going on at your sites?

Qahtani? No, no. It was apples and oranges.

We later see the pictures of Abu Ghraib, which is an indication of some spillover of this sort of lack of discipline, I guess you'd say.

I don't know. It was damaging. It was not just damaging; it was damaging to the country, damaging to the government.

And helpful to Al Qaeda.

Yes. It was also, I think, damaging to the agency by implication. I think there was a tendency around this period of time. Details about the CIA program were slowly but surely leaking out. I think there was a conflation among some members of public, frankly some members in the media, and frankly some politicians to conflate that —

Isn't that conflation partly the fault of the CIA for keeping so much secret?

Well, CIA by nature is a secret organization. I don't know how one can blame CIA, that has responsibility for conducting covert actions, for not purging forth with all of their covert actions.

No, but an interrogation program could have been more transparent than it was.

I think the one mistake, the major mistake we made—and I played a role in this—is that we should have from the beginning briefed more members of Congress, from the get-go, about our interrogation program, about the techniques. We should have laid them all out.

What did instead happen was that for the first five years of the program, pursuant to orders from the White House, we only were permitted to brief the senior leaders of Congress.

That was pursuant to orders from the White House? Is that from the vice president's office?
It was from the White House.

In real life, that kind of order comes from the White House. In my experience, it wouldn't have been the first time the White House issued a limited notification like that.

So they were saying, "Keep this under the radar"?
And I think that was a mistake, because for five years, I think we should have brought more members of Congress into the loop. So I do accept some responsibility for that.

You take responsibility for that because you advised keeping it secret?
No, but I think not just I but other senior members at the agency who had been around for a while should have pushed back at the White House earlier and harder that we simply needed to tell more [Congress]people about what was becoming an increasingly controversial and frankly leaked program anyway.

Right. Well, you can only keep secrets so long. And as too many people know the secrets, then it's going to leak.
That's the conundrum. But my perception was, it was leaking already.

You've got a discredited program to begin with, and now a guy is coming out with a book, an FBI agent who was on the ground, interviewed some of the high-value detainees, and he's coming out and saying not only was it inhumane, it didn't work. This is going to stir things up. And on top of that, the CIA has heavily redacted certain chapters of the book after their review. This is not a healthy situation for the agency and its reputation. So what would you advise the agency at this point?
Well, this program, frankly, has not proved to be a healthy thing for the agency over the years.

But it was a good program in your view?
It was a good, good program. It was well run. It was carefully run.

And made us safer?
Made us safer. And had there been an easier or less politically risky or less legally risky way to have proceeded, believe me, we wouldn't have resisted.

This was a collective judgment at the agency from the professionals at the beginning that this admittedly aggressive course of conduct was the only viable way to acquire the information needed both to prevent another catastrophic attack on the homeland, but let's also not forget, as the Obama administration acknowledged grudgingly after the death of bin Laden, that the CIA interrogation program played a role in helping the trail that led to bin Laden's end.

How do you know in an interrogation that the information you're getting is good information?
Again, I'm a lawyer, not a professional interrogator. But the program, as I understood it, there was no information that was acted upon or validated as highly reliable unless it had been or could be corroborated by some other source.

The case of Ibn Al-Sheikh Al-Libi is brought to mind. This was a case when somebody was whisked away and interrogated and produced dubious information.
Yes, well, unfortunately I'm still precluded from talking about that case, so you'll have to bear with me on that.

But generally speaking, and this is out in the public, [there have] been many who have concluded that this information [that came from him about the presence of weapons of mass destruction in Iraq] was false; that that information derived was false, led us to war, and in some people's opinion should be a warning that tough interrogations might not always produce reliable information. In theory, is this a cautionary tale?

Again, I am not going to get into that particular case. But I think as a general matter, the history and the evolution of the CIA detention and interrogation program is a cautionary tale, and the cautionary tale being no matter for an agency that was heavily criticized in the wake of 9/11 for being risk-averse, as 9/11 receded inevitably in its shock and horror, the agency, like a lot of entities of government, became subject to political winds it could not control.

The political winds that they couldn't control meaning?
Meaning that actions that were not only viewed as necessary and justified in the early month and years of 9/11 subsequently became, as time went on and the image of 9/11 receded, became politically and legally controversial, and that the agency was subject to—as some of us always thought we would—to these political pendulum swings.

And I think these things did do harm to the agency and [to] people in the agency who never had any intention other than to do the best job, to operate within the law, to perform a critical mission to protect the country. …

Were the people that were brought in to interrogate Abu Zubaydah knowledgeable about Islamic extremism, about Al Qaeda in particular, as far as you knew?
As far as I knew, the interrogation team was a mixture. There were some professional interrogators, but there were also on the scene CIA experts in Al Qaeda, in Islamic fundamentalism, in the life and times of Abu Zubaydah.

One of the claims that Soufan is making is that the FBI had many people who had been looking at Al Qaeda for many years and knew a lot about the organization. And those people were kept out of key interrogations and were not allowed access. Therefore they couldn't apply their expertise in their style of interrogation, and therefore opportunities were lost.
Well, I certainly don't dispute the fact that FBI has considerable expertise in Al Qaeda, so I'm not gainsaying that at all. The FBI

leadership, by choice, understandably and legitimately decided that once the enhanced interrogation program was approved, it could no longer participate in the interrogations of Abu Zubaydah.

And Khalid Sheikh Mohammed and Ramzi bin al-Shibh?
Any of them.

But at times people were let in. In the case of Soufan, he was let in to talk to Ramzi bin al-Shibh, but then he was put aside. He was allowed to interrogate a number of people in Guantanamo, and then he was put aside. He's saying opportunities were lost to connect dots that only an experienced, knowledgeable expert in Al Qaeda and Islamic extremism could have done.
And let me understand this: And Mr. Soufan says only Mr. Soufan could have discerned that?

No. In fact, he says that in the case of Khalid Sheikh Mohammed, he wasn't that familiar with KSM per se, but there was another person inside the FBI who was an expert, who had specialized in studying KSM, and that that person was not allowed to interrogate KSM because it was a decision of the CIA.
Well, that's false.

I just told you where the decision came from to not have FBI personnel participate in interrogations of [high-value] detainees.

You're saying it was the FBI's decision?
It was an FBI decision. It was a legitimate decision. Had the FBI chosen to participate, the CIA would not have objected. It would not have surprised me that there would be time to time where an FBI official would come to one of our facilities, maybe have an opportunity to observe. All of that is entirely possible, entirely proper. …

Well, let's say it was the FBI's decision to stand down. But it was certainly somebody's decision to start up the program and to apply the physical coercion on KSM. And what Soufan would be

saying is that they shouldn't have rushed it. He's going further. He's saying not only should they have not done it, they were ineffective. If you have to waterboard somebody 183 times, how effective is waterboarding?

Again, he's entitled to his opinion.

What about that argument? If you have to waterboard somebody so many times, is that evidence that it's working or that it's not working?

Someone would not be waterboarded any longer or any more times than the experts on the ground determine was necessary to get the person to agree and break down his resistance. Waterboarding wasn't done as a technique or abuse or punishment—

I'm not positing that, and I don't think he is either. But he's asking whether or not the fact that someone is waterboarded dozens or scores of times is evidence of it being effective or ineffective?

Well, I think in the case of KSM, it was a case of having an extraordinarily tough, brutal, resistant figure.

But finally good intelligence was derived?

Valuable intelligence was derived from KSM, from Abu Zubaydah, from the other detainees who were subjected to these techniques. Again, whether that intelligence could have been derived without these techniques, I do not know. And to this day, I think it's unknowable.

I believe strongly that that would not have happened, because we're talking about the most hardened, the most determined and the most knowledgeable of the Al Qaeda leaders.

I simply can't accept that they would have succumbed to a normal question-and-answer period to provide the information they provided, and surely not in anything close to the time frame that the country deserved and needed in those first fear-stricken months and years after 9/11.

What Ali Soufan is saying is, look, there's no scientific method to interrogation; that it has to be individually crafted; that the right key for one detainee doesn't work for with another. That's his complaint about these enhanced interrogation techniques, because they pose a science that if you do one thing to somebody long enough, they'll talk. He says, no, you have to treat each one differently and that you get them to talk because you get them to trust you, and you get a rapport, and therefore they talk.

Let me say that each of the detainees was treated as an individual. There wasn't a checklist of "These are the techniques you will use on all detainees." The list of techniques that was approved was all-inclusive. For a number of detainees, very few of the actual enhanced interrogation techniques were employed.

Of all of the high-value detainees, waterboard[ing] was only employed on three of them. So if the notion is that this was a cookie-cutter approach, that all of these techniques were handed out seriatim, no matter who was sitting in the chair, again, it simply is not true, and it betrays a lack of knowledge about how this CIA program was actually conceived and carried out. ...

Do you have regrets about the program?

No, no. I continue to believe that the program was necessary and effective and that there was no practical alternative other than the one we chose. I can't think of a single thing I could have done or would have done differently.

So no, I have no regrets certainly about my actions. Again, it became, I suppose inevitably, a politically controversial and to some extent damaging thing for the agency, and that's unfortunate. ...

We Shouldn't Try to Work Around The International Ban on Extreme Forms of Interrogation

William Taft IV

William Howard Taft IV has served in the United States government under the administrations of Ronald Reagan, George H.W. Bush, and George W. Bush.

The first question to be addressed here is what the law is with regard to torture, at least as it applies to the United States and the United States government; the second, the question of the efficacy of coercive interrogation techniques.

It is now settled that at least two provisions apply to the question of the lawfulness of using coercive interrogation techniques in wartime. One is the Convention against Torture, which the United States joined some years ago after careful consideration of some of the very difficult issues involved in that subject.[1] The second is Common Article 3 of the Geneva Conventions, which the Supreme Court found applied to the people whom we have taken into custody in the war that the terrorists have declared against us and to the conflict that is ongoing with those terrorist organizations.[2]

The Convention against Torture of course bans all things that are torture. There is a question of whether it applies to actions by the U.S. government outside of the United States, with some people arguing that the prohibition on torture is limited to what is prohibited by the Constitution and that the Constitution does not apply to aliens outside of the United States.[3] That is not a significant position, however. Most of the parties to the Convention, and I believe that includes all the signatories, except us, would say that it

Excerpt from "Legal Standards and the Interrogation of Prisoners in the War on Terror," by Cynthia Arnson and Philippa Strum, Woodrow Wilson International Center for Scholars, December 2007. Reprinted by permission.

does apply everywhere to the actions of the U.S. government. That has been our government's position generally, notwithstanding this argument.

The question has often been raised about whether torture is prohibited under the Convention against Torture in the case of a ticking time bomb: whether you could torture a person when you want to find out where the bomb is from somebody who presumably knows. I think the answer is that the Convention against Torture makes no such exception. The issue is not a new one; it was before the Congress and the government when we signed and ratified the Convention against Torture. The exception simply is not there.

Common Article 3 is a little more extensive. It sets the minimal standard for treatment, and bans cruel treatment. It also prohibits torture of persons in your custody as well as humiliating and degrading treatment.

Of course, how to define "torture," "humiliating and degrading treatment," and "cruel" need to be elaborated. This was reflected in the discussions preceding passage of the Military Commissions Act last year.[4] There was an assertion by the government, in seeking to decriminalize violations of Common Article 3, that Article 3 contained too vague and subjective a standard for deciding what was humiliating and degrading. I do not think that is a fair criticism. Until then, the government had taken a position in the *Army Field Manual* as to what could and could not be done, and as to what was humiliating or degrading.[5] In addition, over the years the United States has not had a great deal of difficulty identifying humiliating and degrading treatment when our own soldiers have been subjected to it.

It may be that these terms were too vague for a criminal statute, but I think that the *Army Field Manual* contains a fairly good set of guidelines as to which coercive techniques of interrogation are and are not permitted for prisoners detained under the law of war.

On the question of the efficacy of torture, I would like to share an anecdote. Last week, the temporary cap on one of my teeth came off and the dentist made a quick temporary repair. When he squirted some air on the nerve, I realized that there were things that I would be glad to tell him, if he agreed to stop doing that—things that I perhaps would not tell him if he were not doing it. That gave me some sense that coercion is effective, at least in my case, for eliciting information that I would not otherwise share.

It is also obviously true, however, that the use of torture is an extreme form of coercion. Its effectiveness is going to be highly dependent on the individual with whom you are dealing, on what he actually knows or does not know, and on the information that you are trying to elicit from him. Perhaps there are more sophisticated techniques available today, but I recall reading about Jesuits in the 16th and 17th centuries who suffered the most excruciating pain but never recanted or did whatever it was hoped that they would do. I am sure that there are people of that sort today for whom torture or the worst kind of coercion will not work. There are other people who give in immediately. I remember that in Bernard Shaw's play of the same name, St. Joan says, "If you hurt me I will say anything you like to stop the pain. But I will take it all back afterwards; so what is the use of it?" This was of course a declaration of faith rather than a providing of information.

These examples underscore the relevance of the particular individual with whom you are dealing and the high variability of the effectiveness of coercive techniques. The law does ban certain coercive techniques, and the *Army Field Manual* has over the years established the use of certain methods of interrogation that do not come to the level of coercion. These include methods such as deception (telling detainees that you know things that you do not know or you are not sure about), pretending to be a detainee's friend, and pretending to be annoyed with him or her. The *Manual* outlines all sorts of techniques that have proven to be effective over the years. The fact that the law does prohibit coercion suggests that there is a general feeling that torture and coercive methods are not effective. The *Army Field Manual* says as much in its preamble, stating that it is believed that coercive methods are less effective in obtaining important information from people in custody than the other methods it suggests should be used.

An obvious problem is that one cannot do it both ways with a single individual. You can never know what you would have gotten out of someone if you had tortured him when you did not, or had used a coercive method when you did not.

I have no doubt that there are some people who have information and will share it under torture, as I would have in the dentist's chair. There are some who will share false information, and there are some who have no information to share. How we deal with that is something that we resolved under the Geneva Conventions and under the *Army Field Manual* guidelines. My own preference would have been to leave things where they were and not look to new methods.

Notes

1. Presidential Decision Directive-39 (PDD-39): "Terrorism Incident Annex to the Federal Response Plan," Feb. 7, 1997, available at http://www.fas.org/irp/offdocs/pdd39_frp.htm; Jim Hoagland, "Pricey Rendition," *The Washington Post*, July 3, 2005.

2. "The Clinton Administration's Policy on Critical Infrastructure Protection: Presidential Decision Directive-63," May 22, 1998, available at http://www.fas.org/irp/offdocs/paper598.htm.

3. Dana Priest, "Wrongful Imprisonment: Anatomy of a CIA mistake," *The Washington Post*, Dec. 4, 2005.

4. Douglas Jehl and David Johnston, "Rule Change Lets C.I.A. Freely Send Suspects Abroad to Jails," *The New York Times*, Mar. 6, 2005; Daniel Benjamin, "5 Myths about Rendition (and That New Movie)," *The Washington Post*, Oct. 20, 2007.

5. Dana Priest, "CIA Holds Terror Suspects in Secret Prisons, Debate Is Growing Within Agency About Legality and Morality of Overseas System Set Up After 9/11," *The Washington Post*, Nov. 2, 2005.

Even If Torture Did Work, It Would Still Be Illegal

Rebecca Gordon

Rebecca Gordon teaches in the philosophy department at the University of San Francisco. She is the author of Mainstreaming Torture: Ethical Approaches in the Post-9/11 United States.

What a scam! Noam Scheiber and Patricia Cohen described it this way in a front-page *New York Times* report on how a small group of incredibly wealthy Americans funded their way into another tax universe: "Operating largely out of public view— in tax court, through arcane legislative provisions and in private negotiations with the Internal Revenue Service—the wealthy have used their influence to steadily whittle away at the government's ability to tax them. The effect has been to create a kind of private tax system, catering to only several thousand Americans."

Yes, you read that correctly: tiny numbers of Americans live on a different tax planet from the rest of us. They've paid for the privilege, of course, and increasingly for the political class that oversees how our country runs. They've insulated themselves in a largely tax-free zone that ensures their "equality" before the law (such as it is) and your deepening inequality before the same— and before them. Their actions have garnered them the ultimate in impunity. In this election season in a country of more than 300 million people, for instance, a mere 158 families (and the companies they control) are putting their (largely tax-free) dollars where our mouths once were. By October, they had provided almost half the money thus far raised by presidential candidates in a move meant to ensure that American democracy becomes their system, their creature. ("Not since before Watergate have so

"Tomgram: Rebecca Gordon, American War Crimes, Yesterday, Today, and Tomorrow," by Rebecca Gordon, TomDispatch.com, January 7, 2016. Reprinted by permission.

few people and businesses provided so much early money in a campaign, most of it through channels legalized by the Supreme Court's *Citizens United* decision five years ago.")

My dictionary defines "impunity" simply enough as "exemption from punishment, penalty, or harm." That's a striking trait for those who lord it over us. In the most incarcerated nation on Earth, with close to 25% of the globe's prison population, there are seemingly no bars strong enough to hold our economic elites or, for that matter, their national security brethren.

The U.S. national security state, like the billionaire class, has grown ever richer and become ever more entrenched in these years, while similarly extracting itself from what was once the American political and legal system. Its officials now exist in a world of secrecy in which, in the name of our "safety," ever fewer of their acts are open to our scrutiny. They inhabit what can only be thought of as a crime-free zone. No act they commit, no matter how extralegal or illegal, will evidently ever land them in a court of law. They have, in essence, total impunity. It doesn't matter whether you're talking about the CIA's massive, extralegal operation to kidnap "terror suspects" (often enough, as it turned out, innocent civilians) and deliver them to the torture chambers of brutal allies or to a system of "black sites" off the coast of normal justice. Lying to Congress, hacking congressional computers, and assassinating American citizens have all been green-lighted. No one was ever punished. When necessary, in the secret corridors of power, officials of the national security state simply mobilize lawyers to reinterpret the law of the land to their taste.

When it comes to impunity, their record has been the equal of anything the billionaire class has done. And none of it was more impressive, in its own way, than the use of obviously illegal methods of torture, euphemistically termed "enhanced interrogation techniques," against helpless prisoners in a secret global prison system, as *TomDispatch* regular Rebecca Gordon reminds us today. You want war crimes? Post-9/11, Washington could have sported the logo: War Crimes "R" Us. If you want to understand what this sort of impunity means in terms of the politics of 2016, then read on.

America Revisits the Dark Side: Candidates Compete to Promise the Most Torture and Slaughter

They're back!

From the look of the presidential campaign, war crimes are back on the American agenda. We really shouldn't be surprised, because American officials got away with it last time—and in the case of the drone wars continue to get away with it today. Still, there's nothing like the heady combination of a "populist" Republican race for the presidency and a national hysteria over terrorism to make Americans want to reach for those "enhanced interrogation techniques." That, as critics have long argued, is what usually happens if war crimes aren't prosecuted.

In August 2014, when President Obama finally admitted that "we tortured some folks," he added a warning. The recent history of U.S. torture, he said, "needs to be understood and accepted. We have to as a country take responsibility for that so hopefully we don't do it again in the future." By pinning the responsibility for torture on all of us "as a country," Obama avoided holding any of the actual perpetrators to account.

Unfortunately, "hope" alone will not stymie a serial war criminal—and the president did not even heed his own warning. For seven years his administration has done everything except help the country "take responsibility" for torture and other war crimes. It looked the other way when it comes to holding accountable those who set up and ran the CIA's large-scale torture operations at its "black sites" around the world. It never brought charges against those who ordered torture at Guantánamo. It prosecuted no one, above all not the top officials of the Bush administration.

Now, in the endless run-up to the 2016 presidential elections, we've been treated to some pretty strange gladiatorial extravaganzas, with more to come in 2016. In these peculiarly American spectacles, Republican candidates hurl themselves at one another in a frenzied effort to be seen as the candidate most likely to ignore the president's wan hope and instead "do it again in the future." As a result, they are promising to commit a whole range of crimes, from torture to the slaughter of civilians, for which the leaders of some nations would find themselves hauled into international court as war criminals. But "war criminal" is a label reserved purely for people we loathe, not for us. To paraphrase former President Richard Nixon, if the United States does it, it's not a crime.

In the wake of the brutal attacks in Paris and San Bernardino, the promises being openly made to commit future crimes have only grown more forthright. A few examples from the presidential campaign trail should suffice to make the point:

- Ted Cruz guarantees that "we" will "utterly destroy ISIS." How will we do it? "We will carpet bomb them into oblivion" -- that is, "we" will saturate an area with munitions in such a way that everything and everyone on the ground is obliterated. Of such a bombing campaign against the Islamic State, he told a cheering crowd at the Rising Tide Summit, "I don't know if sand can glow in the dark, but we're going to find out." (It's hard not to take this as a reference to the use of nuclear weapons, though in the bravado atmosphere of the present Republican campaign a lot of detailed thought is undoubtedly not going into any such proposals.)
- Kindly retired pediatric neurosurgeon Ben Carson evidently has similar thoughts. When pressed by CNN co-moderator Hugh Hewitt in the most recent Republican debate on whether he was "tough" enough to be "okay with the deaths of thousands of innocent children and civilian[s]," Carson replied, "You got it. You got it." He even presented a future campaign against the Islamic State in which "thousands" of children might die as an example of the same kind of tough love a surgeon sometimes exhibits when facing a difficult case. It's like telling a child, he assured Hewitt, that "we're going to have to open your head up and take out this tumor. They're not happy about it, believe me. And they don't like

me very much at that point. But later on, they love me." So, presumably, will those "dead innocent children" in Syria— once they get over the shock of being dead.

- Jeb Bush's approach brought what, in Republican circles, passes for nuance to the discussion of future war crimes policy. What Washington needs, he argued, is "a strategy" and what stands in the way of the Obama administration developing one is an excessive concern with the niceties of international law. As he put it, "We need to get the lawyers off the back of the warfighters. Right now under President Obama, we've created... this standard that is so high that it's impossible to be successful in fighting ISIS." Meanwhile, Jeb has surrounded himself with a familiar clique of neocon "advisers"—people like George W. Bush's former Deputy Secretary of Defense Paul Wolfowitz and his former Deputy National Security Advisor Stephen Hadley, who planned for and advocated the illegal U.S. war against Iraq, which touched off a regional war with devastating human consequences.
- And then there is Donald Trump. Where to start? As a simple baseline for his future commander-in-chiefdom, he stated without a blink that he would bring back torture. "Would I approve waterboarding?" he told a cheering crowd at a November rally in Columbus, Ohio. "You bet your ass I would —in a heartbeat." And for Trump, that would only be the beginning. He assured his listeners vaguely but emphatically that he "would approve more than that," leaving to their imaginations whether he was thinking of excruciating "stress positions," relentless exposure to loud noise, sleep deprivation, the straightforward killing of prisoners, or what the CIA used to delicately refer to as "rectal rehydration." Meanwhile, he just hammers on when it comes to torture. "Don't kid yourself, folks. It works, okay? It works. Only a stupid person would say it doesn't work."

Only a stupid person—like, perhaps, one of the members of the Senate Intelligence Committee who carefully studied the

CIA's grim torture documents for years, despite the Agency's foot-dragging, opposition, and outright interference (including computer hacking)—would say that. But why even bother to argue about whether torture works? The point, Trump claimed, was that the very existence of the Islamic State means that someone needs to be tortured. "If it doesn't work," he told that Ohio crowd, "they deserve it anyway."

Only a few days later, he triumphantly sallied even further into war criminal territory. He declared himself ready to truly hit the Islamic State where it hurts. "The other thing with the terrorists," he told Fox News, "is you have to take out their families, when you get these terrorists, you have to take out their families. They care about their lives, don't kid yourself. When they say they don't care about their lives, you have to take out their families." Because it's a well-known fact—in Trumpland at least—that nothing makes people less likely to behave violently than murdering their parents and children. And it certainly doesn't matter, when Trump advocates it, that murder is a crime.

The Problem with Impunity

Not that you'd know it in this country, but the common thread in all of these proposed responses to the Islamic State isn't just the usual Republican hawkishness. Each one represents a serious violation of U.S. laws, international laws of war, and/or treaties and conventions that the United States has signed and ratified under Republican as well as Democratic presidents. Most campaign trail discussions of plans—both Republican and Democratic—to defeat ISIS have focused only on instrumental questions: Would carpet bombing, torture, or making sand glow in the dark work?

Candidates and reporters alike have ignored the obvious larger point—if, that is, we weren't living in a country that had given itself a blanket pass on the issue of war crimes. Carpet-bombing cities, torturing prisoners, and rendering lands uninhabitable are all against the law. They are, in fact, grave *crimes*. That even critics of these comments will not identify such potential acts as war crimes can undoubtedly be attributed, at least in part, to the fact that no one—other than a few low-level military personnel and a CIA whistleblower who spoke publicly about the Agency's torture agenda—has been prosecuted in the U.S. for the startling array of crimes already committed in the so-called War on Terror.

President Obama set the stage for this failure as early as January 2009, just before his first inauguration. He told ABC's George Stephanopoulos that, when it came to the possible prosecution of CIA officials for U.S. torture policies, "We need to look forward as opposed to looking backwards." He didn't, he assured Stephanopoulos, want the "extraordinarily talented people" at the Agency "who are working very hard to keep Americans safe… to suddenly feel like they've got to spend all their time looking over their shoulders and lawyering up." As it turned out, lawyering up was never a problem. In the end, Attorney General Eric Holder declined to charge any CIA personnel, closing the only two cases the Justice Department had even opened. Nor did any of the top officials responsible for the "enhanced interrogation" program, including President George W. Bush, Vice President Dick Cheney, Secretary of Defense Donald Rumsfeld, or CIA Director George Tenet, need to waste a cent on a lawyer. Instead, they're now happily publishing their memoirs. Or, in the cases of Jay Bybee and John Yoo, the Justice Department authors of some of the more infamous "torture memos," serving as a federal judge or occupying an endowed chair at the University of California, Berkeley, School of Law, respectively.

On December 1, 2015, perhaps driven to frustration by the Obama administration's ultimate failure to act, Human Rights Watch (HRW) released a 153-page report titled "No More Excuses." In it, the organization detailed the specific crimes relating to that CIA torture program for which a dozen high-level officials of the Bush administration could have been brought to trial and called for their prosecution. HRW pointed out that such prosecutions are not, in fact, a matter of choice. They are required by international law (even if the alleged criminals have run the planet's last superpower).

For example, the United Nations Convention against Torture, a key treaty that the United States signed in 1988 (under President Ronald Reagan) and finally ratified in 1994 (under President Bill Clinton), specifically requires our nation to take "effective legislative, administrative, judicial, or other measures to prevent acts of torture in any territory under its jurisdiction."

It doesn't matter if there's a war on, or if there's internal unrest. The Convention says, "No exceptional circumstances whatsoever, whether a state of war or a threat of war, internal political instability or any other public emergency, may be invoked as a justification of torture."

Whenever torture is used, it's a violation of that treaty, and that makes it a crime. When it's used against prisoners of war, it's also a violation of the 1949 Geneva Conventions and therefore a war crime. No exceptions.

But when Obama acknowledged that "we tortured some folks," he claimed an exception for American torture. He cautioned us against overreacting. "It's important for us not to feel too sanctimonious in retrospect about the tough job that those folks had," he said, referring to the CIA's corps of torturers. He pointed to American fear—of the very sort we're seeing again over San Bernardino—as an exculpatory factor, reminding us of just how frightened all of us, including CIA operatives, were in the days after 9/11.

As it happens, whatever the former constitutional law professor in the White House or hotel-builder Donald Trump may believe, torture remains illegal. It makes no difference how frightened people may be of potential terrorists. After all, it's partly because people do wicked things when they are afraid that we make laws in the first place—so that, when fear clouds our minds, we can be reminded of what we decided was right in less frightening times. That's why the Convention against Torture says "no exceptional circumstances whatsoever" excuse such acts.

But the U.N. Convention is just a treaty, right? It's not really a *law*. In fact, when the United States ratifies a treaty, it becomes part of American law under Article VI of our Constitution, which states that the Constitution itself and

> ... all treaties made, or which shall be made, under the authority of the United States, shall be the supreme law of the land; and the judges in every state shall be bound thereby, anything in the Constitution or laws of any State to the contrary notwithstanding.

So even if torture did work, it would still be illegal.

War Crimes for the New Year

What about the other proposals we've heard from Republican candidates? Some of them are certainly war crimes. "Carpet bombing," a metaphor that describes an all-too-real air-power nightmare (as many Vietnamese, Laotians, and Cambodians learned during our wars in Indochina), means the saturation of an entire area with enough bombs to destroy everything standing without regard for the lives of anyone who might be on the ground. It is illegal under the laws of war, because it makes no distinction between civilians and combatants.

Because aerial bombardment hadn't even been invented in 1907 when the Hague Conventions were signed, they don't name carpet bombing specifically in a list of prohibited "means of injuring the enemy, sieges, and bombardments." Nevertheless, at the center of the Hague Conventions, as with all the laws and customs of war, lies the crucial distinction between combatants and civilians. To destroy an entire populated area in order to eliminate a handful of fighters violates the long-held and internationally recognized principle of proportionality.

The Hague Conventions also put into the written international legal code long-held beliefs about the importance of distinguishing between civilians and combatants in war. Ben Carson's willingness to allow the deaths of thousands of civilians and children in the pursuit of ISIS fundamentally violates exactly that principle.

In another shameful exception, the United States has never ratified a 1977 addition to the Geneva Conventions that specifically outlaws carpet bombing. Additional Protocol 1 specifically addresses the protection of civilians during warfare. Apart from such U.S. allies as Israel and Turkey, 174 countries have signed Protocol 1, explicitly making carpet bombing a war crime.

If the United States has not ratified Protocol 1, does that mean it is free to violate its provisions? Not necessarily. When the vast majority of nations agree to such an accord, it can take on the power of " international customary law"—a set of principles that have the force of law, whether or not they are written down and ratified. The International Committee of the Red Cross maintains a list of these rules of law. One section of these explicitly states that "indiscriminate attacks," including "area bombardment," are indeed illegal under customary law.

Senator Cruz's promise to discover whether or not sand glows in the dark, presumably through the use of nuclear weapons, would violate the 1907 Hague Convention's prohibitions on employing "poison or poisoned weapons" and on the use of "arms, projectiles, or material calculated to cause unnecessary suffering." It no more matters that the United States ratified this convention over a century ago than that the Constitution is more than 200 years old. Jeb Bush's suggestion that we get the lawyers "off the back of the warfighters" notwithstanding, both remain the law of the land.

That they don't appear to have the force of law in the United States, that the description of possible future war crimes can rouse crowds to a cheering frenzy in this political season, represents a remarkable failure of political will; in particular, the willingness of the Obama administration to call a crime a crime and act accordingly. Globally, it is a failure of power rather than of the law. Prosecuting a former African autocrat or Serbian leader for war crimes is obviously a very different and far less daunting matter than bringing to justice top officials of the planet's only superpower. That is made all the more difficult because, under George W. Bush, the United States informed the world that it would never ratify the accords that set up the International Criminal Court.

In the Glare of San Bernardino

Human Rights Watch released its report on December 1st. The next day, a married couple, Syed Rizwan Farook and Tashfeen Malik, attacked a holiday party at San Bernardino's Department of Public Health, where Farook worked. They killed 14 people before dying in a police shootout. It was a horrific crime and it appears that the two were, at least in part, inspired by the social media presence of the Islamic State (even if they were not in any way directed by that group). Not surprisingly, the HRW report sank like a stone from public view. With it went their key recommendations: that a special prosecutor be appointed to investigate and bring to trial those responsible for CIA torture practices and that U.S. torture victims be guaranteed redress in American courts, something both the Bush and Obama administrations have fought fiercely, even though it is a key requirement of the U.N. Convention against Torture.

As last year ended, the fear machine had cranked up once again, and Americans were being reminded by those who aspire to lead us that no price is too high to pay for our security -- as long as it's paid by somebody else. Expect more of the same in 2016.

And yet it is precisely now, when we are most afraid, that our leaders—present and future—should not be stoking our fears. They should instead be reminding us that there is something more valuable—and more achievable—than perfect security. They should be encouraging us not to seek a cowardly exception from the laws of war, but to be brave and abide by them. So here's the challenge: Will we find the courage to resist the fear machine this time? Will we find the will to prosecute the war crimes of the past and prevent the ones our candidates are screaming for? Or will we allow our nation to remain what it has become: a terrible and terrifying exception to the international rule of law?

Organizations to Contact

The editors have compiled the following list of organizations concerned with the issues debated in this book. The descriptions are derived from materials provided by the organizations. All have publications or information available for interested readers. This list was compiled on the date of publication of the present volume; the information provided here may change. Be aware that many organizations take several weeks or longer to respond to inquiries, so allow as much time as possible.

Amnesty International
5 Penn Plaza, 16th Floor
New York, NY 10001
212-807-8400
email: aimember@aiusa.org
website: https://www.amnesty.org

Amnesty International campaigns for a world where human rights are enjoyed by all. Amnesty International states that torturers will become international outlaws. Their website contains news, reports, and a database of archived articles, including a number of pieces on enhanced interrogation, one that even calls for the arrest and prosecution of former US president George W. Bush for violating international torture laws.

Brookings Institution
1775 Massachusetts Avenue NW
Washington, DC 20036
202-797-6000
email: communications@brookings.edu
website: www.brookings.edu

The Brookings Institution is a nonprofit public policy organization that conducts independent research. The Brookings Institution uses its research to provide recommendations that advance the goals of strengthening American democracy, fostering social welfare and security, and securing a cooperative international system. The organization publishes a variety of books, reports, and commentary that deal with the numerous issues, including enhanced interrogation.

Cato Institute
1000 Massachusetts Avenue NW
Washington, DC 20001-5403
202-842-0200
website: www.cato.org

The Cato Institute is a public policy research organization dedicated to the principles of individual liberty, limited government, free markets, and peace. The institute publishes numerous policy studies, two quarterly journals, *Regulation* and *Cato Journal*, as well as the bimonthly *Cato Policy Report*.

Center for American Progress (CAP)
1333 H Street NW
Washington, DC 20005
202-682-1611
website: www.americanprogress.org

The Center for American Progress (CAP) is an independent nonpartisan policy institute that is dedicated to improving the lives of all Americans through bold, progressive ideas, as well as strong leadership and concerted action. CAP develops new policy ideas, challenges the media to cover the issues that truly matter, and shapes the national debate. CAP publishes the ThinkProgress blog.

Center for National Security Studies (CNSS)
1730 Pennsylvania Avenue NW, 7th Floor
Washington, DC 20006
202-721-5650
e-mail: cnss@cnss.org
website: www.cnss.org

The CNSS is an advocacy organization that serves as a watchdog in defense of civil liberties, human rights, and constitutional limits on government power. CNSS works to prevent illegal or unconstitutional government surveillance, combat excessive government secrecy and strengthen public access to information, and assure more effective oversight of intelligence agencies.

Council on Foreign Relations (CFR)
58 East 68th Street
New York, NY 10065
212-434-9400
email: communications@cfr.org
website: www.cfr.org

CFR is an independent, nonpartisan organization, think tank, and publisher dedicated to being a resource for its members, government officials, business executives, journalists, educators and students, civic and religious leaders, and other interested citizens in order to help them better understand the world and the foreign policy choices facing the United States and other countries.

Human Rights First
75 Broad Street, 31st Floor
New York, NY 10004
Tel: 212-845 5200
email: info@humanrightsfirst.org
website: www.humanrightsfirst.org

Human Rights First is an independent advocacy and action organization that challenges America to live up to its ideals. Around the world, Human Rights First works where it can best harness American influence to secure core freedoms.

Human Rights Watch
350 Fifth Avenue, 34th floor
New York, NY 10118-3299 212-290-4700
email: hrwpress@hrw.org
website: www.hrw.org

Human Rights Watch is a nonprofit, nongovernmental human rights organization with offices around the world. Human Rights Watch meets with governments, the UN, regional groups, financial institutions, and corporations to press for changes in policy and practice that promote human rights and justice around the world.

National Security Agency (NSA)
9800 Savage Road
Fort Meade, MD 20755-6248
301-688-6524
website: www.nsa.gov

The National Security Agency (NSA) provides information to US decision makers and military leaders. The NSA coordinates, directs, and performs activities that protect American information systems and produce foreign intelligence information. The NSA provides speeches, briefings, and reports on public information on its website.

The United Nations
405 East 42nd Street
New York, NY, 10017
(212) 963-9999
email: inquiries@un.org
website: www.un.org

Currently made up of 193 member states, the United Nations is an international organization established to take action on the issues confronting humanity in the twenty-first century, such as peace and security, climate change, sustainable development, human rights, disarmament, terrorism, humanitarian and health emergencies, gender equality, governance, food production, and more.

Bibliography

Books

Jared Del Rosso. *Talking About Torture: How Political Discourse Shapes the Debate*. New York, NY: Columbia University Press, 2015.

Bill Harlow. *Rebuttal: The CIA Responds to the Senate Intelligence Committee's Study of Its Detention and Interrogation Program*. Annapolis, MD: Naval Institute Press, 2015.

J. Porter Harlow. *How Should We Treat Detainees?: An Examination of "Enhanced Interrogation Techniques" Under the Light of Scripture and the Just War Tradition*. Phillipsburg, NJ: P & R Publishing, 2016.

Marouf Arif Hasian, Sean T. Lawson, and Megan McFarlane. *The Rhetorical Invention of America's National Security State*. Lanham, MD: Lexington Books, 2015.

Michael Kerrigan. *The Instruments of Torture*. London, UK: Amber Books, 2017.

Tracy Lightcap. *Politics of Torture*. New York, NY: Palgrave Macmillan, 2016.

Tracy Lightcap and James P. Pfiffner. *Examining Torture: Empirical Studies of State Repression*. New York, NY : Palgrave Macmillan, 2014.

Alfred W. McCoy. *Torture and Impunity: The U.S. Doctrine of Coercive Interrogation*. Madison, WI: The University of Wisconsin Press, 2012.

James E. Mitchell and Bill Harlow. *Enhanced Interrogation: Inside the Minds and Motives of the Islamic Terrorists Trying to Destroy America*. New York, NY: Crown Forum, 2016.

Samantha Newbery. *Interrogation, Intelligence and Security: Controversial British Techniques*. Manchester, UK: Manchester University Press, 2015.

James E. Pfander. *Constitutional Torts and the War on Terror*. New York, NY: Oxford University Press, 2017.

John Anthony Rizzo. *Company Man: 30 Years of Controversy and*

Crisis in the CIA. Brunswick, Vic.: Scribe Publications, 2014.

Jose A. Rodriguez and Bill Harlow. *Hard Measures: How Aggressive CIA Actions After 9/11 Saved American Lives*. New York, NY: Threshold Editions, 2012.

John W. Schiemann. *Does Torture Work?* New York, NY: Oxford University Press, 2016.

Marc A. Thiessen. *Courting Disaster: How the CIA Kept America Safe and How Barack Obama Is Inviting the Next Attack*. Washington, DC: Regnery Pub, 2010.

United States and Dianne Feinstein. *The Senate Intelligence Committee Report on Torture: Committee Study of the Central Intelligence Agency's Detention and Interrogation Program*. Brooklyn, NY: Melville House Publishing, 2014.

Anna M. Wittmann. *Talking Conflict: The Loaded Language of Genocide, Political Violence, Terrorism, and Warfare*. Santa Barbara, CA: ABC-CLIO, 2017.

Periodicals and Internet Sources

J.M. Arrigo, D. DeBatto, L. Rockwood, and T.G. Mawe. "The 'Good' Psychologist, 'Good' Torture, and 'Good' Reputation—Response to O'donohue, Snipes, Dalto, Soto, Maragakis, and Im (2014) 'the Ethics of Enhanced Interrogations and Torture'" *Ethics & Behavior*. 25.5. 2014. 361-372.

Myles Balfe. "Standardizing Psycho-Medical Torture During the War on Terror: Why It Happened, How It Happened, and Why It Didn't Work." *Social Science & Medicine*. 171. 2016. 1-8.

Myles Balfe. "Why Did U.S. Healthcare Professionals Become Involved in Torture During the War on Terror?" *Journal of Bioethical Inquiry : an Interdisciplinary Forum for Ethical and Legal Debate*. 13.3. 2016. 449-460.

J. Beynon. "'Not Waving, Drowning.' Asphyxia and Torture: the Myth of Simulated Drowning and Other Forms of Torture." *Torture: Quarterly Journal on Rehabilitation of Torture Victims and Prevention of Torture*. 22. 2012. 25-9.

M. Chwastiak. "Torture As Normal Work: the Bush Administration, the Central Intelligence Agency and 'enhanced Interrogation Techniques'" *Organization*. 22.4. 2015. 493-511.

I. Greenberg. "From Surveillance to Torture: the Evolution of Us Interrogation Practices During the War on Terror." *Security Journal.* 28.2. 2015. 165-183.

Douglas A. Johnson, Alberto Mora, and Averell Schmidt. "The Strategic Costs of Torture: How 'Enhanced Interrogation' Hurt America." *Foreign Affairs.* 95.5, 2016: 121-132.

Alexandra King, "CIA contractor: Enhanced Interrogation Techniques 'Saved Lives.'" CNN. December 20, 2016. http://www.cnn.com.

J.D. Mayer and D.J Armor. "Support for Torture Over Time: Interrogating the American Public About Coercive Tactics." *Social Science Journal.* 49.4. 2012. 439-446

W. O'Donohue, C. Snipes, G. Dalto, C. Soto, A. Maragakis, and S. Im. "The Ethics of Enhanced Interrogations and Torture: a Reappraisal of the Argument." *Ethics and Behavior.* 24.2. 2014. 109-125.

William O'Donohue, Alexandros Maragakis, Cassandra Snipes, and Cyndy Soto. "Psychologists and the Ethical Use of Enhanced Interrogation Techniques to Save Lives." *Ethics and Behavior.* 25.5. 2015. 373-385.

J.W. Schiemann. "Interrogational Torture: or How Good Guys Get Bad Information with Ugly Methods." *Political Research Quarterly.* 65.1. 2012. 3-19.

"These Are The 13 Enhanced Interrogation Techniques The CIA Used On Detainees." Associated Press, Dec. 10, 2014. http://www.businessinsider.com.

Nina K.Thomas. "Gaslighting, Betrayal and the Boogeyman: Personal Reflections on the American Psychological Association, Pens and the Involvement of Psychologists in Torture." *International Journal of Applied Psychoanalytic Studies.* 14.2 2017. 125-132.

J. Zahora. "Between Sovereignty and Biopolitics: The Case of Enhanced Interrogation Techniques." *Perspectives.* 22, 87-109.

Steven Michael Ziegler "Did the C.I.A.'s Enhanced Interrogation Techniques Violate International Law?" Journal of Law and International Affairs at Penn State Law. May 23, 2015. https://sites.psu.edu.

Index